FIGHTERS FOR PEACE

ALBERT I
King of Belgium

FIGHTERS FOR PEACE

BY
MARY R. PARKMAN

**ILLUSTRATED WITH
PHOTOGRAPHS**

Essay Index Reprint Series

Originally Published by
THE CENTURY CO.
NEW YORK

BOOKS FOR LIBRARIES PRESS
FREEPORT, NEW YORK

INTERNATIONAL STANDARD BOOK NUMBER:
0-8369-2439-8

LIBRARY OF CONGRESS CATALOG CARD NUMBER:
73-167399

PRINTED IN THE UNITED STATES OF AMERICA
BY
NEW WORLD BOOK MANUFACTURING CO., INC.
HALLANDALE, FLORIDA 33009

To C. W.

Whose generous assistance and
exacting criticism made possible the preparation
of these sketches

CONTENTS

LIST OF ILLUSTRATIONS

THE CHAMPION OF HONOR:

KING ALBERT OF BELGIUM

"If it is necessary for us to resist an invasion of our soil, that duty will find us armed and ready to make the greatest sacrifices. . . . I have faith in our destinies. A country which defends itself wins the respect of all, and cannot perish."

KING ALBERT OF BELGIUM.

FIGHTERS FOR PEACE

THE CHAMPION OF HONOR

A T first it did not seem as if Destiny had picked him out for a king. His older brother was the heir presumptive, and nobody dreamed that a lad so vigorous would not live to reign. Prince Albert, therefore, was permitted to go quietly and happily along through his childhood without "the fierce light which beats upon a throne" dazzling or bewildering his young spirit.

He was born in April, 1875, in the palace of the Rue de la Regence in Brussels, but of all the royal houses where he spent part of his time, he loved the château of Amerois best. It was beautiful living on a hilltop, with a quaint old town that seemed like a story-book village nestling at its foot, and the ancient Ardennes forest for a playground. The terrace was a free, skyey place, where by day he could look out across the green valley of the Semois to the distant pine-covered hills, and where at night he could in a moment

3

slip far away from the world into a wonderful tent of stars.

The days seemed made for delight in the splendid park of the château, where one could ramble over the hillside, cooled by the spray of silver streams cascading down to the valley, or loiter and dream in the green and gold paradise among the friendly trees. Within doors, too, life was full of charm. There were the great halls with pictures of people, his own people—kings and princes about whom his mother told him wonderful stories. But when he was still a little boy he learned to look upon the library where his father loved to spend his days as the best place of all. Here one could in a moment through the magic of a book find wings for his spirit and slip away to distant lands or far-away times where there were all sorts of interesting people and things to think about.

But there were many real people coming and going all the time, who made him think and wonder too. There was his uncle, the King, who often used to look at him and his brother in a strange, dark way that filled him with awe. "The one who rules a nation has many cares," his father explained. "Besides, your uncle still grieves over

4

the loss of his boy. He may think it is strange that I have two tall, strong boys, while his only son was not permitted to grow up to take his place as king." But most of their friends—princes and counts, not only of Belgium but also royal cousins from other countries—seemed to find life one happy holiday.

Perhaps Prince Albert would have taken it for granted that the world was made for enjoyment if he had not seen very early another, darker side even at the forest château. There were poor, unhappy people, many of them, who came to their door with tales of trouble and want. He often saw his mother's eyes fill with tears as she talked to these people, and he knew that she never turned any one away without help. But still he wondered about it all. It was strange that some children should have everything and others have nothing at all.

He went one day to his father with his question. "It does n't seem right that so many people should have to *beg* for what they need from others who have so much more than enough," he said. "Is n't there some way that all can have a fair chance to help themselves?"

The Count of Flanders looked up from his book

5

and regarded the boy thoughtfully. A man of many gifts, he had, because of growing deafness, given up his claim to the throne and all part in public affairs. His books were the chief joy and solace of his days.

"You are wondering about a thing that has puzzled many wise heads and kind hearts for a long time," he said. "It has always been a world of rich and poor."

"Yet," insisted the Prince, "that does n't prove that it always must be so, does it? Surely we might make things a little better."

"Yes, my boy, that is what the King is working for all the time—to build up trade that will make Belgium more prosperous," his father replied.

"Perhaps I can help, too, one of these days," said Albert.

This talk set him to thinking. Surely a prince was in honor bound to serve his people in every way. "A prince must be one who is able and ready to lead," he said to himself. "Otherwise he has no excuse for being, nor has loyalty any meaning. I must set about learning the things that will make me know how best to be useful to my country."

"I want to read the books that tell about wealth

and poverty, and the ways of managing the affairs of a country in the best way," he said one day to his tutor.

"I suppose you refer to political economy and sociology," replied the teacher. "I was planning to introduce you to those serious sciences when you are a little older."

"I think I am ready now," said the Prince.

So it was that the boy began early to think about the subjects which claimed much of his serious study in later years. Of course he knew he was to be a soldier—all princes were born to the army —but there would be time for much besides soldiering. However, when at sixteen he was ready to enter the Belgian Military School, his life had suddenly changed. His older brother, Prince Baudouin, had died, and as heir to the throne he found that his training had become a matter of special concern. The King, himself, presented him to his teachers and classmates, and his speech of introduction was a great ordeal, for Leopold II, tall, commanding, and much given to unexpected shafts of wit, was an awe-inspiring person even to those of his own family.

However, Prince Albert soon won a place for himself among his fellows, as one of them. It did not take them long to perceive that the tall, lanky youth, who did not know what to do with his newly acquired inches or his hands and feet, was as shy as themselves; and that, moreover, he was a genuinely good fellow both in the class-room and on the playground. In trying to put the awkward boy at his ease, they forgot to stand in awe of the future king.

The Belgian Military School was a thoroughly democratic institution. In the case of only a crack regiment or two were the officers members of the nobility. A uniform did not carry social prestige, and, since the army was notoriously un-derpaid, there was little inducement for ambitious youths to adopt a military career. Besides, no-body took the service very seriously. A neutral country like Belgium was by its treaties absolved from the necessity of being prepared to protect itself, people said.

The soldiers were recruited in a very curious fashion—by a draft from which any one who drew a bad number might get his release by paying for a substitute. Only the very poorest could not, by borrowing or otherwise, muster enough money to secure exemption from a service that would encroach upon their best earning years. The

8

ranks of the privates, then, were filled by the patriotic few who did not believe in the substitute system, and the unfortunate many, who were so poor that they had been willing, as the officers said, "to sell their skin." For these latter, Prince Albert did not share the contempt of his mates, and he treated all the men with a uniform friendliness which showed that even in his thought he made no distinction.

"The men are in most cases no more to blame for their poverty than they are for our abominable system of recruiting," he said. "If I am ever king I shall see that Belgium has a real army that rests on the service of all her sons. A nation must be able to defend itself in order to respect itself and to win the respect of others."

King Leopold II had been striving valiantly to bring about this reform, in spite of the indifference of the great mass of the people. His very last act was to sign a law that went far toward bringing about a better order of things, and King Albert's first work after coming to the throne was to carry his plans to completion by introducing general military service.

"When the people stand shoulder to shoulder they will know each other better," said Prince

9

Albert to himself, "and they will feel that they are all Belgians, forgetting the differences between Flemings and Walloons."

For little Belgium is as a nation very young, having been created in 1830 by international politics to help maintain the balance of power. Its population is made up of two distinct races—the Walloons, a Latin people speaking French; and the Flemings, a branch of the Teutonic family whose tongue is much like that of the Dutch. French was the official language of the country, and for a long time the Flemish speech and ways were regarded as a mark of inferiority; for, while the Flemings outnumbered the Walloons, they belonged for the most part to the humbler classes. With the growth of industry and commerce, however, many of this despised race rose to wealth and influence, and, discovering that they belonged to a people quite as old and honorable as the haughty Walloons, they demanded equal chance for the preservation of their language and traditions. This rivalry grew; and when King Albert began his reign it was commonly said that there were no Belgians, only Walloons and Flemings.

"I must from the first be the King of all my

people," he said; "only in that way can I help them to feel that we are truly one nation."

So it was that when, in 1909, King Albert addressed his parliament for the first time, he took the oath both in Flemish and French. As the last words sounded through the noble Belgian Chamber: "I swear to myself and to the country to fulfil scrupulously my duties, and to consecrate all my forces and all my life to the service of our native land"—the people gathered there were exalted, thrilled. It was the first time that the Flemish tongue had been heard in that place, but it was not so much of that they were thinking now as of their king himself. Of course they might have known he would do it; had he not as prince always done what was fair and right in little things and great? Albert was every inch a king, and his reign would be both good and glorious, they thought, as they looked at the tall figure, the fair, noble face, and earnest, kindly blue eyes. *"Vive le Roi! Vive Albert!"* the shout went up on every side, and there was heartfelt affection as well as loyalty in the cry.

As a prince, Albert had endeared himself to the people by his efforts to improve the condition

11

of the poor. His interest in problems of political economy and social service had grown and borne fruit. "The rich and great can take care of themselves," he used to say; "it must be my task to help the poor to help themselves." He made a journey to America to learn about conditions of workers in the new world; in particular, under the friendly guidance of James J. Hill, he made a serious study of railroads. In England, disguised as a newspaper reporter, he lived for a time trying to glean some knowledge of the conditions under which the shipbuilders and fishermen worked.

"I never see a machine or a motor without wanting to know the *what* and *how* of it," he once said. In following up this native interest, he gained an astonishing practical knowledge of the construction of ships, automobiles, and airplanes. He could on occasion mend his own machine or act as his own chauffeur. And knowing machines gave him something that he longed to possess —a real understanding of the men who must do the machine work of the world.

Not content with these efforts to know his own people, the Prince sought to get some personal knowledge of the savages of the Congo Free State who were dependent on Belgium. For, since Leopold II had provided Stanley with the means of exploring this vast territory of central Africa, it had come under the absolute control of the King, and he in turn had willed his interest to his country. "I must know about that part of my job as King of Belgium," said Albert to himself, determined to see for himself the condition of the savages, who, it was said, were grossly ill-treated by native taskmasters, put in control by the Belgian rubber merchants.

In 1909, therefore, Albert set out for Africa and spent three months traversing the dense forests and tropical jungles of that savage country, walking in all some fifteen hundred miles. Everywhere the blacks gathered about in happy excitement to see the "Tall Man, Breaker of Stones," as they called him. "I am not the King," he said; "I cannot do everything. But I have come here because I want to know you, and find out what we in Belgium can do to help you."

The day of Prince Albert's return to his country was an occasion of great rejoicing. The people of every party vied with each other in doing honor to the Prince who had been preparing himself to rule by learning how to serve.

The Prince's marriage, nine years before the Congo trip, had also been a time of public jubilation. . . . On a visit to Munich he had become acquainted with Princess Elizabeth of Bavaria, daughter of a man to whom the ability to serve his people meant more than the power and place he had inherited from his royal forebears. A famous oculist who spent his days in a hospital, Duke Charles Theodor had brought up his two daughters to feel that there is nothing more royal than service. Both had passed through the regular hospital training as nurses, and Elizabeth had, moreover, taken the full medical course. The young Belgian prince was at once drawn to this family whose ideas of kingly privileges were so like his own; and it was not long before Belgium was thrilled by the news that their prince was to marry Princess Elizabeth.

"Was there ever a more beautiful royal romance!" they said; and, when they saw their future queen, fair, dainty and appealing,—"Was there ever a lovelier princess!" For all felt at once that she was quite the fairy-book heroine— "good as she was beautiful"; and who could doubt that the romance would have the correct

14

fairy-book ending: "They lived happy ever after"?

Any one who saw King Albert on his coronation day, riding at the head of his staff, would have said, looking from the noble, commanding figure in the general's uniform to the fine, earnest face, "He will be a king indeed—in peace or in war." And any one who saw the carriage drawn by six horses—quite in the fairy-book manner—where rode their beloved queen and the two young princes, Leopold and Charles, with the King's mother, the Countess of Flanders, would have said that there was nothing wanting in the happiness of the royal family.

Among King Albert's brother monarchs who accompanied him on that gala day was Wilhelm of Hohenzollern; and again in April, 1910, the German Emperor made a point of visiting Belgium to assure the people of his warm regard:

"Full of amiable sympathy, I, in common with all Germany, observe the surprising success which the Belgian people has won in all the domains of commerce and industry. . . . May the reign of your Majesty spread happiness and prosperity amongst your royal house and among your people. This is the profound wish of my heart, with which

15

I cry, Long live their Majesties, the King and Queen of the Belgians!"

When the German army entered Brussels four years later, they found copies of this speech posted on every side; but these were, of course, only annoying "scraps of paper," which were soon torn down and thrust out of sight.

King Albert had, two years before the German invasion, been warned by one of his royal kinsmen that the Kaiser did not intend to regard the treaty guaranteeing the neutrality of Belgium, but that he was making plans to attack France through that country. This warning made it clear that Belgium, in spite of the solemn pledge of the great nations, might need in desperate earnest an army of defense; but King Albert's plans for its organization were only realized in part when the storm broke. On August 2, 1914, the King received the German ultimatum, demanding that Belgium allow the Imperial army free passage through its territory on penalty of being regarded as an enemy.

Now, in a moment, the heroic character of king and people was revealed to the world. To the great nation whose minister had just declared that their treaty was a mere "scrap of paper" which

16

they would naturally disregard since "necessity knows no law," the little defenseless country sent this reply: "The German ultimatum has caused the Belgian people deep and painful astonishment; and Belgium refuses to believe that her independence can only be preserved at the cost of violating her neutrality."

When, on that fateful day of August, 1914, King Albert, the champion of honor, stood before his parliament, there was a moment of suspense. Would the different parties stand together in this dark hour? Would the soldier-king have a united country at his back? As the King looked about him at the representatives of the people his words rang out manfully:

"If a stranger should violate our territory he will find all the Belgians gathered around their Sovereign, who will never betray his constitutional oath. I have faith in our destinies. A country which defends itself wins the respect of all, and cannot perish. God will be with us."

For a moment there was a hush and then a great rallying cry. Belgium was one in its resolution to fight for its honor to the last. Party rivalry was forgotten; and the saying "Flemish and Walloon are only Christian names; Belgian is our family name" proved more than idle words.

It was impossible for the Germans to realize how any intelligent people could be so foolish as to stand out for an idea—for a mere word, like *honor*—when every instinct of prudence and common sense bade them submit to the nation that had the power to make good its threats.

"Oh, these poor, stupid Belgians!" cried the German minister with tears in his eyes. "Why don't they get out of the way! I know what it will be. I know the German army. It will be like laying a baby on the track before a locomotive!"

The world knows how bravely the hastily mobilized, half-equipped little army fought at Liége; how, as the shield of France and of civilization, they held back the invading host until the Allies were able to organize their forces for defense. Hoping against hope that help would come in time to save Brussels, they fought with the strength of desperation. Then the King decided to withdraw the armed force from both Brussels and Louvain, in order to save if possible their historic buildings and monuments from destruction. At Antwerp a last stand was made.

Think of what that tragic retreat meant to the King who had dreamed of leading a peaceful nation into ways of prosperity and contentment. Behind him he saw fields of golden grain trampled under foot, homes burned, churches destroyed, women and children homeless and helpless. Those who saw his face in those days knew that his heart was heavy with the sorrows of all his people.

For a brief breathing space Antwerp was spared; and then the Germans, failing to take Paris, fell back on the Belgian city for the consolation of a minor success. Then it was that King Albert retreated to the tiny corner of land near the sea-coast that was for four years all that remained of free Belgium. Here in that land of dikes and dunes, they opened the sluice gates, letting in the sea to help stay the advance of the enemy. And for four years the brave Belgians kept their line in the flooded country, holding back 200,000 Germans and guarding the coast passage to Calais.

Can you picture the staunch, uncomplaining little Belgians at their posts amid mud and water, wading up to their knees in passing from one line of defense to another? Of course digging in was impossible. They selected a spot of high ground, such as a railroad embankment, and made themselves barricades of sand bags, which had to be rebuilt again and again as they were scattered by the enemy fire or melted down by the rain. After a man had been plunging about for three or four hours bringing sand for parapets and reeds for camouflage his clothes became so weighted with mud that he could scarcely move. His heart within him, too, must have been heavy indeed as he thought of his home destroyed, his harvest for which he had toiled seized by the Germans, his family scattered—cold and hungry, perhaps, at that very moment. All that he could see as he looked about him was a ghostly gray land of flood and mist, with a farm or two rising here and there like half-submerged islands. This was all that remained to Belgians of their smiling, fertile country. Yet King Albert's soldiers were always cheerful.

"There is only one thing that counts," said a Belgian officer, "to stand by our king until victory comes. For win we must. . . . Did they show you the site of that German villa on the beach which covered a cemented platform for a gun that could have raked Nieuport? That place was planned strategically and built long before the war—at a time the Kaiser was congratulating us on our prosperity. Do you think that the war-makers

20

will find that there is no god but brute force?''

In the spirit that says, ''We await the end,'' the Belgians rallied about their leader who shared their fortunes from first to last. Many stories are told of his visits to the advance lines, of his heartening words to the soldiers, of the way he had been known to seize the gun and drop into the place of a man who had been hit. He never left his army or the bit of Belgian soil that remained to him except for brief visits to the leaders of the Allied forces in France.

And Queen Elizabeth never left his side except for flying visits to her children in England. The *''bonne petite reine,''* (good little queen), as the people call her, was from the first in charge of ambulance and hospital work at the front. Daily she visited the Ocean Ambulance, comforting and cheering the sick and wounded as well as directing the nurses.

''One can see the hand of Providence in my early training that prepared me to meet this need,'' she said simply.

A little summer villa between the sand dunes and the sea at the fishing village of La Panne was for months the home of the King and Queen. Here they were together when the King was not

at his headquarters or with his troops. With
hostile airplanes circling overhead and cannon
ceaselessly booming in the distance, there was
never a time when they could, in the sound of the
eternal wash of the waves, forget the tragedy of
the present hour.

Slowly but surely, however, the scene changed
on that dismal Belgian front. Above the gray
flooded waste masses of waving reeds sprang up,
where gulls, ducks, and other water birds hovered
about. Kindly Nature strove to reclaim the war-
blasted land even while the work of destruction
went on. And man, too, had wrought changes.
Foot-bridges were laid across the water separat-
ing the various lines of defense, and wonderful
camouflage screens of reeds covered the roads and
the stations of the machine guns. The men, too,
had developed a hardihood of body and mind that
was proof against discomforts and difficulties.

A famous cartoonist made a drawing showing
King Albert standing amid the ruins of his country, confronted by the Kaiser who taunted him
in this wise: "You see you have lost everything!" "Not my soul!" replied the Belgian
King. . . . Even in the darkest days when Belgium seemed utterly at the mercy of the invaders,

THE CHAMPION OF HONOR

who carried off her treasures, destroyed her means of industry, put to death many of her people and deported many more to work in the land of the oppressor,—even then the unconquerable soul of the nation was marching on to a sure triumph.

For the conscience of the world was with Belgium, and all the free peoples of the earth were aroused. Thousands of men from across the sea came to take up the battle. The King who had stood as the champion of honor was the leader, not only of his own brave nation, but of a mighty host from many lands. Victory was sure.

On November 22, 1918, King Albert entered Brussels at the head of his army, followed by French, English and American troops. Flowers were thrown in his way. The joy of the people knew no bounds; it seemed as if the dawn of peace and the great day of freedom of the nations had come. The bells of Belgium could peal out from her steeples, ringing out the sad time of cruelty and oppression, ringing in the new day when there should be no fear that even the chimes of her churches would be seized to make cannon for the enemy.

As the King rode by on horseback with his two young sons—the Crown Prince in khaki and

23

the Count of Flanders as a midshipman—a father lifted his little boy to his shoulder that he might see over the surging crowd.

"This is a great day, my son," he said, "but I remember a greater. It was the day the King stood before the representatives of the people and, speaking for them, said that come what might, Belgium would be faithful to her word and the trust of the nations. That was the real moment of victory."

THE HERO OF THE MARNE:

MARSHALL JOFFRE

Give us a name to stir the blood
With a warmer glow and a swifter flood,—
A name like the sound of a trumpet, clear,
And silver-sweet, and iron-strong,
That calls three million men to their feet,
Ready to march, and steady to meet
The foes who threaten that name with wrong,—
A name that rings like a battle-song,—
  I give you *France!*

HENRY VAN DYKE.

THE HERO OF THE MARNE

WE are told that a certain man who feared that his ambition might sleep never to wake, bade his servant say each morning as he let the light of the new day into his bed-room, "Remember that you have great things to accomplish!" Most of us know how easy it is for the many little things that make up our every day lives to crowd out all thought of the big things that we hope to do some time. We realize that we need many reminders and much urging to arouse the sleepy will within.

But the boy who grew to be the great general that all the world honors as the savior of France —Marshal Joffre, the Hero of the Marne—needed no one calling from without to say, "Be strong; be ready! Your country will need you some day." There was a voice within that was never silent saying, "There is work to be done. Be ready!"

Joseph Joffre's wide blue eyes were steady and thoughtful. "He never seems to have time for any fun," complained one of his school-mates.

"You can't tell anything about him," said another. "There was never such a fellow for holding his tongue!"

Young Joffre certainly had the habit of silence. When a boy is the oldest of eleven children and knows that he has been chosen from among them all to go to a school where officers for the army are trained, he knows that the business of commanding his own days is a serious matter.

His father, Gilles Joffre, was a cooper who was well known and respected in that countryside of southern France where vineyards cover every sunny slope. Years after when one of the wine merchants wished to give the highest praise to a cooper, he would say, "That is a barrel as good as Gilles Joffre used to make." It was as if one said of a violin, "It is a Strad!"

There came a day in 1867 when the cooper took his son, then an awkward lad of fifteen, to a school in Paris. As he turned to go, leaving him to the new life in the strange, big world, he gave Joseph a long look. There was every question in his eyes. If the boy's steady blue ones did not give the answer sought, the firm grasp in which he took his father's work-worn hand was more eloquent than any words could have been.

THE HERO OF THE MARNE

Paris was the gayest city in all the world at that time when the Emperor, Napoleon III, was trying to make his reign seem great and splendid by every sort of extravagance and display. It was hard to believe that the carefree days and the nights brilliant with fêtes could ever come to an end. Life was surely made for enjoyment. Even in the school for civil and military engineers where Joseph Joffre was a student the holiday spirit often threatened to interfere with the serious concerns of the days of study. All the glitter of the gayest capital in Europe could not, however, lure the cooper's son from his appointed tasks.

There is a story that when he was a very small school-boy he had often been known to build a wall of books about him on his desk to shut away the merry faces of his companions when they threatened to be more interesting than his arithmetic and drawing. In these days in Paris, however, there was no need of building any sort of material barricade about his study table.

"It would have been a bold fellow who would have thought of laying siege to Joffre when he was intent on a problem. There was something about him that made one think of an impregnable fortress," said a retired officer who had been at the Polytechnic when the great general was a student there.

There came a day when the thought of the people of Paris turned as in a moment from trifles and business and gayety to the forts about the city. The Prussians were at the gates; the gay capital was plunged in all the horrors of a siege. Joffre, then a lad of eighteen, served as junior subaltern in one of the forts. He fought bravely through the siege by the side of other brave Frenchmen but he had to suffer with them the grief of seeing his beloved country defeated and forced to give up her fair provinces of Alsace and Lorraine together with a vast sum of money to add to the menacing power of the enemy.

Now the companions of the silent hard-working subaltern began to see that his devotion to long mathematical problems was not without result. A certain awe-inspiring Field-Marshal stopped one day before the section of the fortifications that had been constructed under that quiet young officer's direction.

"I congratulate you, Captain!" he exclaimed in a burst of unaccustomed enthusiasm. Joffre's serious dreams had taken shape in stronger walls for Paris, and the young engineer of twenty-four had been made a captain.

Captain Joffre went on with his work as a builder of defenses, now about Paris, now in the Pyrenees, now in Madagascar or in China. Wherever his country sent him he pitched his tent and worked upon her fortifications and entrenchments as if life held nothing else for him.

"My brother was always lost in thought," said his sister. As the child's play had been lost in the study of the ambitious boy, so now the ambitions of the man were lost in the love of his work for its own sake.

One summer while spending a brief vacation with his father, he made a journey to a famous fort which he fell to examining with the eager interest of the expert. The corporal of the battery viewed with angry concern the behavior of the stranger in civilian dress.

"He is a German spy!" he exclaimed, and promptly ordered his arrest. Captain Joffre, too intent on the problems that had challenged his attention to make any protest, suffered himself to be led before the officer in charge, where his identity was soon made evident.

"Why did you not tell the corporal who you were?" he was asked on his return home.

"I was thinking of the fort," he replied simply.

All this time Joseph Joffre was in training for his days of generalship, building defences against defeat by his thorough preparedness. While he planned fortifications and laid foundations for heavy guns that should withstand the assaults of the enemies of his country, he was unconsciously fortifying himself to meet emergencies by learning to recognize opportunities when they appeared, as they so often do, disguised as difficulties and failures. And his secret was only that of hard work. Some one has said, "Three-fourths of any fact is the *act* that is in it." Joffre's success in mastering facts lay always in his capacity for instant, instinctive, and untiring effort.

Have you heard the story of the conquest of Timbuktu, the mysterious fortified city near the southern border of the Sahara desert which was for many years the centre of the native trade in gum, rubber, gold and ivory? But the white men of many nations who braved the dangers of Central Africa to barter beads, bright colored cloth, and various articles of iron and steel for these products of the land did not dare to penetrate the

JOSEPH-JACQUES-CÉSAIRE JOFFRE
Marshal of France

country as far as Timbuktu. Their commerce was at best uncertain and hazardous.

The French longed to plant a colony in Africa that should make trade safe so that the people of the world might enjoy some of the gifts that Nature had hidden away in the unexplored Dark Continent. It was certain that this could be done only by conquering Timbuktu, the stronghold of the hostile, treacherous tribes.

An expedition was put in command of Colonel Bonnier, a brilliant, dashing officer who was in every way the ideal figure of a conquering hero. He chose Commandant Joffre to lead the supporting force of a thousand men who were to furnish reserves and bring along the provisions and ammunition. "Joffre is steady and prudent; we know we can depend on him," said the leader.

There came a day when a hunted remnant of Colonel Bonnier's men fled to join Joffre's small band. Their leader had been overwhelmed by a sudden attack that found him unprepared, and he, with eleven of his officers, had been slain. The panic-stricken survivors thought only of retreat and escape, but Joffre quietly took command and led a successful march through desert waste and jungle, bristling with enemies, to Timbuktu. Out of a company of a thousand men, two-thirds of whom were porters and laborers, together with the survivors of the first expedition, Joffre organized a fighting unit who forged ahead with a morale that spelled success, ready at any moment to forestall sudden assaults and to meet the enemy in battle array. "One may surprise, but to be surprised is simply criminal," he said.

They tell us that during this time he went for days without sleep. One of his eyes, was, moreover, stung by a poisonous insect and became terribly inflamed, but even that did not compel him to relax his watchfulness.

"How can I direct my troops blindfolded?" cried Joffre when the doctor of the party declared that he might lose his sight if he did not wear a bandage.

"Then you must put on blue glasses," ordered the doctor.

"I will when I find a pair growing by the way," said Joffre.

Do you believe that "there is a Providence that shapes our ends," or do you prefer to think that a blind Chance is responsible for the wonderful things that happen? The glasses *were* found by the way. A package that had been sent to one of the officers of the party contained a pair of blue spectacles which probably saved the leader's brave blue eyes from total blindness. Look at any good picture of the Marshal and you will see that a film veils the left eye. That tells the story of the injury and his narrow escape.

On February 12, 1894, Timbuktu, called "the mysterious," fell before Commandant Joffre who was within the month made Lieutenant Colonel. All the world knew that the French flag was flying over the dreaded stronghold of the fiercest of African tribes, but few could have told you anything about the quiet leader who had turned defeat into victory. He did not have the dash that seizes the fancy of the crowd and he never talked about himself. He was content to let his deeds speak.

"Well, Gilles, is your son a general?" the neighbors would say to the old cooper.

"No, but he's a colonel," was the staunch reply.

Then, one day in 1901, the little town of Rivesaltes could say with the proud cooper, "My son is a general!"

He was not a "big, brass general" whose glitter of uniform and important manner blared out "See the conquering hero comes!" whenever he appeared. The humble neighbors of that town in the Pyrenees who knew how to judge the simple, enduring things of life—the ways of the ripening harvest, the coming of autumn to the mountains, and the power of hard-working men to toil on, trusting that the future would reward faithful effort—felt that this leader, who went on as quietly with his studies as he had when a subaltern, would be a commander that the country could trust in its hour of need. It was one such unlettered but understanding man, a sergeant who had served under Joffre in the Far East, who said at the time that General Joffre was made Commander-in-Chief of the French army, "When Joffre is in command there is no need to worry. Success is assured. That man Joffre is a veritable wolf-trap for the enemy."

What would have supported the people of France through the terrible days of September, 1914, when the German army was sweeping on towards Paris and Joffre's forces were falling back in retreat if they had not had this faith, firm but silent, in "the man who never spoke," as the quiet General was often called?

Those were days of cruel suspense when the French army was day by day giving ground, precious soil of France, to the mercy of the invader. Think of the distress of the people in the towns and villages whose homes were destroyed by cannon. Picture the anxiety of the people of Paris, of all those who could do nothing but wait and hope. Can you imagine the suspense of the army, Joffre's own soldiers, when day after day the order came to retreat, still to retreat?

Those who saw General Joffre in those days knew as they met his deep, steady gaze that he felt the distress of all the people as his own, but his look of quiet power was unchanged. In reply to the question of one of his staff he said in his customary calm, even tones:

"I mean to deliver the big battle in the most favorable conditions, at my own time and on the ground I have chosen. If necessary, I shall continue to retreat. I shall bide my time. No consideration whatever will make me alter my plans."

It seemed that the strength and confidence of the leader were communicated as the very breath of power to his men. They kept their faith in their general and in victory in the midst of apparent defeat. "Papa Joffre" would never fail them.

At last the moment came for which Joffre had been planning. He had by his retreat led the

German armies too far ahead of their supply bases. All eagerness for the final stroke they bounded forward, each command striving to be the first to enter Paris. They forgot that "an army moves on its stomach," and that guns without ammunition are so many straws. They thought that nothing could hold back their invincible troops. Joffre's day had dawned. He knew that the Germans were weary from the long marches, that they were sustained only by the intoxication of success. He knew that his million men, unprepared and unorganized as compared with the million and a half soldiers of the Kaiser, were yet in a position to strike with confidence in the victory.

On the morning of September 5, 1914, the word was sent along the "far-flung battle-line" that the retreat was at an end. All was busy, determined preparation for the great battle for which they had waited and prayed. Everywhere along the front was read the Order of the Day, and it was as if leader and men were clasping hands in mutual understanding and solemn pledge.

"At the moment of engaging a battle on which the fate of the country hangs, it is necessary to remind every one that the time has passed for looking backward. Every effort must be made to attack and to drive back the enemy. The hour has come to advance at any cost, and to die where you stand rather than give way.''

For four days and nights the battle raged. Try to picture the scenes along the front. Battalion after battalion of picked German troops were thrust forward in close formation as if sheer headlong force must win everywhere. Then see the ranks mowed down by the French machine guns and cannon and the rifles of men who were fighting that their beloved France might live. When, on the evening of September 9, the Kaiser was compelled to sign the order for a general retreat of his armies, the Battle of the Marne had been won and the hope of Germany that Paris could be taken and the French conquered by an irresistible onslaught before the surprised nations had chance to pull themselves together for proper defense, was dashed to the ground. The turning-point had come and the tide had changed. The Battle of the Marne will forever rank among the great decisive battles of the world.

Picture the people of Paris who had been waiting breathless for Joffre's hour. There were the old men who could do nothing but hope and pray, leaving the battle to the young men at the front.

There were the women taking up quietly the work
of their husbands and brothers, while their hearts
were hushed in the suspense of longing for news
of their loved ones and the triumph of France.
There were children looking up to the white faces
of their mothers in wonder and dumb questioning.
—What had suddenly happened to the world of
sunshine and happy work and play?

A woman wearing black for her only son had
been kneeling with two little girls in the church
of the Madeleine. As she came out on the portico
she pushed back her veil and looked about her
as if she were gazing into the face of a friend from
whom she feared to be forever parted. There was
love and prayer in her eyes, but also a great sor-
row. At that moment a small boy slipped into
her hand a bit of folded paper on which was written, "We must not despair; France cannot be
beaten." It seemed to her that the words rang
out in the clear, strong tones of her son—her
brave Jean. Quickly she turned to the lad, her
face alight now with hope and courage. She
learned that he and his mother had been busy for
two days and nights in their poor garret writing
hundreds of such messages to carry a word of

confidence to anxious people during that time of
trial.

"We must win while General Joffre leads our
brave army and while Paris has such true hearts
among those who wait at home," she said. And
it seemed to the boy that the smile of that sad
mother and the ring of triumph in her voice would
always stay in his memory.

In a few days the faith of the people in their
leader and in the destiny of France was justified.
All the world was talking of the miracle of the
great victory and sounding the praises of General
Joffre, the Hero of the Marne.

When people spoke to Joffre of his triumph he
said quietly, "It is not the commanding generals
who win the battles. It is rather the colonels and
even the simple captains. When the fighting front
extends over some five hundred or six hundred
miles the will of one man cannot be felt everywhere, for there is but little opportunity for new
combinations and surprises. The rôle of commanding general all but comes to an end the moment he has gathered at a desired point in battle
line the forces that he sees are needed. The rôle
of the colonels and captains begin when the first

shot is fired. They decide the result of the struggle. The troops that win are those that have the faith and courage to hold out longest—that prove superior in endurance, in energy, and in confidence in the final victory.''

People marvelled that Joffre was so unspoiled. ''He never fails to give the other officers and the men in the ranks their share of the credit,'' said a man in blue to a companion in khaki. ''Our army is like one big family. Those Boche captains who drive their men into battle with blows of their swords should see how our men rush forward at a word. We would trust 'Papa Joffre' through everything.''

''Papa Joffre'' seemed to have no ambition. When another might have sought to keep the leader's power and place, he saw that the other generals—Pétain and Foch—should have their turn at the command.

''They will come with fresh power to the great task,'' he said. ''France needs the best that all her sons can bring.''

General Joffre was given the highest honor that his country could confer; he was made Marshal of France. But still the son of the cooper of Rivesaltes was untouched by ambition. His fondest dream was to be allowed to retire after his years of service to his quiet home in the Pyrenees. "The battle must be taken up by younger men," he said. "I shall perhaps have earned my days of rest."

"The Battle of the Marne was the first great triumph of the World War, and the coming of America into the struggle was the second," said a great Frenchman. It was fitting, therefore, that Marshal Joffre should have been chosen to come to America to speak for France to her new ally.

The welcome given to the Hero of the Marne can only be compared to the enthusiastic reception accorded Lafayette on his second visit to the United States. Those who saw him as he stood at salute before the Stars and Stripes, or as he turned to greet the throngs of cheering school children, knew that the hero of the Marne was indeed a great man, true, brave, and single-minded in his devotion to his country and in his forgetfulness of self.

"Your cordial welcome moves me deeply," he said, "because I know it is homage paid to the whole French army which I represent here."

I like to picture the general who saved France at Mount Vernon where he went to place a bronze

43

wreath upon the tomb of the general who won liberty for the United States. "In the French army all venerate the name and memory of Washington," he said. "I respectfully salute here the great soldier and lay upon his tomb the palm we offer to our soldiers who have died for their country."

After returning to France, Marshal Joffre was frequently seen in company with General Pershing, for whom he expressed warm admiration. All that his experience had gained in the three years of fighting was put at the service of the American leader. "Papa Joffre" became known as the "godfather of the American army."

Not long since I saw a boy who had been one of those to give a good account of himself at Château-Thierry. "We'd be pretty poor stuff if we fell down on the job, we fellows who had Marshal Joffre for godfather," he said with a smile that took no account of his empty sleeve.

And so the spirit of the Hero of the Marne marched on winning other victories for freedom.

THE CHEVALIER OF FLIGHT:

CAPTAIN GUYNEMER

A hero of legendary power, he fell in the wide heaven of glory, after three years of hard fighting. He will long remain the purest symbol of the qualities of the race: indomitable in tenacity, enthusiastic in energy, sublime in courage. Animated with inextinguishable faith in victory, he bequeaths to the French soldier the imperishable remembrance which will exalt the spirit of sacrifice and the most noble emulation.

INSCRIPTION TO GUYNEMER IN THE PANTHEON.

THE CHEVALIER OF FLIGHT

OF all the heroes of the World War, Georges Guynemer, the "gallant flying boy" of France, most appeals to the imagination. "A hero of legendary power, he fell in the wide heaven of glory after three years of hard fighting" reads the inscription set up in his memory in the Pantheon, that classic Hall of Heroes in Paris. The very sound of his name enkindles ardor and stirs the heart. He has been called "the knight of the air," "the wingèd sword of France," and the story of his miraculous exploits is already linked with that of Joan of Arc. Like her, he seems to stand for the eager, unquenchable spirit of France.

He was born on Christmas Eve, 1894. "I lead a charmed life," he used to say laughingly when his companions protested that he took too many risks. "You see it is not easy to hurt a chap who was born on Christmas Eve!"

He was a child of frail body and indomitable will. It was as if Fate sought to prove once and for all that spirit was master—that soul could conquer in spite of every physical handicap. See the picture of him, a lad of twelve, among his mates at school. He is slighter and paler than them all, but his dark eyes burn with an intense fire that defies all restraint, all fettering bonds of bodily limitation, and even, we can fancy, knowing the story of the triumph of his brief life, the mortal exactions of Time and Space. . . .

As a tiny lad, he knew that his parents had grave concern because of his health. There were many consultations with physicians; there were journeys in search of health and strength. His education began at home under the governess of his two sisters.

"No doubt it is best," complained his father, a retired army officer, whose fondest dream it was that his only son should win a place among those who serve their country, "but it looks as if we may have one petticoat too many in the family."

There were walks with the father, and many long talks about the glories of the past that their town of Compeigne had shared. The chief enthusiasm of Guynemer *père* was history, and there was not one of the streets where they walked but could furnish a text. Kings had been consecrated there; kings had died there. Treaties that changed the destiny of nations had been signed there. Louis the Grand and the great Napoleon had given splendid fêtes there. . . . But every walk to the palace, the abbey, or to the forest, was somehow incomplete if they did not go by the open square of the Hotel-de-ville, where a maiden in armor stood lifting the standard of France to the sky.

"Who is she?" asked the child.

"Jeanne d'Arc."

Again and again he stood there gazing at the figure of the young girl who had led the armies of her country to victory and crowned her king, as he demanded to hear yet again about the miracle of her short life. It appeared that history was not all made by the wise and prudent like his father, but that children, too, had been able to do glorious things. Something seemed to draw him to that bronze maiden, who stood there straight as a sword, bearing her banner aloft. His heart burned within him, and a whisper came that guided all his days.

"It is not how long we live that matters, but

how and what we live. Life is not measured by
the clock, but by noble heart-beats and brave
deeds.'' . . . The thought became clearer each
time he stopped before the statue of the Maid.
Surely she had lived as much for herself and the
world as any one, no matter how many years and
honors he might have to his credit.

When his father told him the stories of his own
people—how there was a Guynemer among those
about whom the poet sang in the "Song of Roland,'' that men of that name had been among
those who fared forth on the Crusades, and that
ever since, his forbears had been men who had
served their country gallantly, keeping the honor
of their fine, old family bright, again the whisper
came, "It is not how long they lived that counts.
Who cares to know the age of a Roland? The
memory of glorious deeds alone remains.''

At the age of twelve, little Georges Guynemer
entered Stanislas College at Compeigne as a day
pupil. They tell us that he was no book-worm
—that he was too "tameless and swift and proud"
to be held down by routine exercises. His quickness of intelligence and ready wit were recognized,
and his "ambition of the first rank.'' At the
end of the first year, Georges had won first prize

50

in arithmetic, but it was on the playground in games that demanded agility and daring that the slight boy most distinguished himself.

One game known as *la petite guerre* delighted the boy above everything else. The group of boys was divided into two armies, each commanded by a general chosen by themselves. All the soldiers strove to defend bands of color which they wore as armlets, and also to preserve from capture flags which floated from a wall, tree, or some other selected spot. A boy whose armlet was seized was *hors de combat*—a dead soldier. It is interesting to note that the boy who was most lacking in physical strength was a leader in this game. His energy, quickness of eye and wit, as well as his darting swiftness of movement and daring originality of attack, won for him first place. But it is to be noted also that he was never chosen general. His gifts were too much needed in the ranks of those who fought, and besides, he loved the struggle for its own sake. How he delighted in attacking the strongest and the most distinguished scholars of them all, conquering by a sudden turn before the other could tell what was happening;—and then the triumph of bearing the trophies to his general! He had no desire for leadership that would give him a rôle apart and aloof, leaving to others the chances and thrills that belong to the heat of the fray. So Georges Guynemer was always *simple soldat.*

We have here an astonishing likeness of the youth, who, a few years later, was chief among all his country's brave knights of the air, the ace of aces who had fifty-four aëroplanes and two hundred and fifteen combats to his credit. He cared too much for the fight to wish to command. He was the knight of solitary combat, preferring even to go alone in his machine, which he controlled with his feet and one hand while he fired his gun with the other. He attacked always the strongest, daunted neither by the number nor prowess of his antagonists. His quickness and unexpectedness of attack were unequalled. As if to show that life did not depend upon brawn or upon any virtue of physique alone, he conquered in spite of his frail body, proving that the will to do can triumph over every obstacle and overthrow the strongest.

Notwithstanding periods of enforced retirement from his studies to the infirmary, or to his home for a prolonged rest of two or three months, he succeeded in keeping abreast of his class and in graduating at the age of fifteen. The next autumn he returned to go on with his studies in preparation for the Polytechnic, specializing in mathematics and physics. At the same time his native interest in mechanics engaged not only most of his spare time but also many hours stolen from his regular tasks. His room was a veritable curiosity shop, where coils of wire, wheels, chemicals, batteries, and all sorts of mechanical odds and ends were jumbled together with note-books, staid texts, and articles of clothing.

His spirit of invention which had shown itself when he was a child of four or five, now came into play in constructing a telephone that should put him in quick communication with a friend in a distant part of the building. He developed a passion for experimentation in physics and chemistry.

"He was absorbed for hours at a time," said Lieutenant Constantin, a comrade at Stanislas, "in working over problems in mathematics or mechanics, without giving a thought to what went on around. When he had solved the problem that challenged him or had succeeded in discovering something new, he would return satisfied to the affairs of the moment."

A friendship made during these days at school had a great influence on the particular development of his interests. Jean Krebs, son of the manager of the Panhard motor car factory—that Colonel Krebs whose name is associated with the early progress in the production of aerial motors —became young Guynemer's constant companion. The workshop of his room or even the college laboratory was too narrow now. His real school was the motor factory, where he eagerly mastered the fascinating details of workmanship and management of the various engines and mechanical contrivances.

One day during the last year of preparation for the Polytechnic, his father carried him off for a much-needed rest to his grandmother's in Paris, after which he spent some weeks in travel with his mother and sisters. Then, one day, his father drew him apart for a serious talk.

"You have had, my son, your years of preparatory study, and some leisure to think of the future. What profession do you plan to follow?"

Without a moment's pause or change of expression, as if he were not aware of saying something extraordinary, Georges replied, "Aviator."

"But that is not a profession," said the amazed

father. "That is only a sport. You run through the air as an automobilist chases along the highways of the country. Then after spending your best years in the pursuit of pleasure, where are you?"

Then Georges told his father what he had not breathed before to a living soul, not even his friend, Constantin, or Jean Krebs. "I have no other passion. One morning from the quadrangle of the college I saw an aviator fly over high in the air. I cannot explain what happened, but something new took possession of me. I felt a deeper emotion than I have ever known before, a feeling almost religious. You must trust me, my father, when I beg you to let me go with the aëroplanes."

"You do not know what it is that you ask, my boy," replied the father, moved by his son's extraordinary earnestness. "You have no knowledge of a flying machine except from below. It is a far-away romance to you."

"You are wrong," replied Georges, "I have been up in one at Corbeaulieu." Corbeaulieu was an aërodrome not far from Compeigne.

A few months later, in July, 1914, the Guynemers were at Biarritz. Much had happened in the intervening weeks. Georges had been denied admission to the Polytechnic because of his frail health. "He will not live to complete the course," declared the examining professors. It was the first real disappointment of the boy's life—the first closed door. Heretofore he had not felt that his weak body was a particular handicap; his spirit had risen triumphant over every limitation. But now it appeared that others had the power to rule for him, and to prevent his entering the life he felt must be his.

To Biarritz they went for the mellow sunshine and soft sea breezes of the famous resort. Surely such golden days would bring health and strength. There were, however, other possibilities besides loitering on the sands and bathing at Biarritz. The beach made a fine landing-place for aëroplanes. It was not accident, you may be sure, that brought young Guynemer to the spot when one of the great birds swept down to earth. He examined the motor and every detail of the machine; he talked to the pilot. He never doubted that he was born to fly!

But then, as in a day, the gay world of study and adventure was changed. A heavy cloud obscured the sunshine even at Biarritz. His country was plunged in war. In a moment former dreams and longings passed away with the sunshine. Even flying was forgotten as something unreal and far away. Georges stood before his father, breathless with suspense.

"I must enlist," he said.

"It is your right," replied the ex-captain, looking at his son proudly.

"You will permit—"

"I envy you," was the firm answer.

But again a closed door! Three times the youth presented himself, and three times he was refused. They could not see beyond the slight form and the delicate chest, and recognize the spirit that would push on and triumph in real warfare for his country, as the frail child had overcome the strongest at school in the game of war. He felt that life held nothing for him; it seemed that he was helpless to lift himself out of the slough of despond.

Then, one day, a glimpse of his old friend, the gallant Maid who stood as ever, holding aloft the standard of her country, quickened his spirit. She, too, had known the torture of feeling herself held back when all her soul was urging her forward, but she had kept on and saved France. It was not always by strength and might that destiny was shaped. . . . Some solemn words that he had heard chanted in church rang in his ears now with new meaning:

> He hath put down the mighty—
> And hath exalted the humble and meek.—

Was not Joan of Arc an eternal witness to the truth of those words?

As in a flash he saw what he could do. His old dreams revived in a new guise, and he saw the path ahead. He was on the sand when an aëroplane came to earth that day, and he talked earnestly for a moment with the sergeant-pilot.

"How does one enlist in the aviation service?" he asked.

"See the Captain at Pau," was the reply.

The boy's parents hardly recognized him when he next appeared, his face alight with life and hope. Surely the doctors were mistaken; he must get well. It was unthinkable that such youth and fire should be so soon extinguished.

"*Mon père*, I must go to Pau to-morrow," he declared without preamble, "to enlist as an aviator. Before the war you would not listen, but

58

now you see that aviation is more than a sport.''

And the lad had his wish. On the morrow he presented himself before Captain Bernard-Thierry, who was in command of the aviation camp at Pau. It seemed as if his heart would burst, and the eager words fairly tripped over each other.

"My Captain, do me but this favor. Take me in! Employ me at anything at all, even cleaning the machines. You are my last chance. Let it be through you that I am permitted to do something in this war."

The Captain looked at the slender boy with the burning eyes and flushed cheeks. He saw more than the slight form; he divined something of the power of the spirit within. He was a man who believed that the soul is master of the frame in which it dwells.

"I can take you as pupil-mechanic," he said.

Guynemer drew a long sigh. This door at least was not shut. "Good!" he exulted. "I have some knowledge of motors."

That was in November, 1914. After two months as mechanic he had won a place among the ranks of student aviators, and on February first he made his trial trip aloft as pilot. "I began in a 'taxi'" he said, "and then the following week I mounted an airplane, going in straight lines, turning and gliding; and on March 10 I made two flights lasting twenty minutes. At last I had found my wings; I passed the examination next day."

We are told that Guynemer's ambitious spirit almost proved his undoing at the very beginning of his career. The head pilot complained that he was too rash, venturing out in contrary weather and essaying turns that were far too difficult for one of his small experience. Guynemer always shivered slightly when he spoke of how narrowly he had escaped being dropped from the list of military aviators.

It was not long before the master pilot and all the rest of the camp knew that the youth they had so nearly lost was the leader of them all— an eagle among the birds of the air. Though his daring attacks seemed to take no account of risks, he returned victorious from every encounter. As the boy at school in the game of war had always sought to vanquish the strongest, so now the young eagle always marked the flight of the first among the enemy planes and strove to bring those to the ground. Before three weeks had passed, he had brought his fifth Boche plane to the earth, thus becoming an ace.

The splendid abandon and sublime courage of his adventures in the air won the adoring admiration of all his comrades, and accounts of his exploits were passed eagerly from mouth to mouth. The story of the combat of September 29, 1916, moved all France, and the young aviator awoke to find himself the hero of the hour. Seeing one of his comrades attacked by five enemy planes, he mounted to the rescue. At a height of 10,000 feet, he shot and sent to earth two within thirty seconds of each other. The others tried to escape, but pursuing, he brought down a third in two minutes. Then—a mischief!—a shell exploded under his machine tearing off one of the wings of the noble bird. Down he fell into No Man's Land where in an instant he was seen rising from the wreck. The enemy opened up a diabolical machine gun fire to prevent his escape, but with a mighty shout the French surged "over the top" and succeeded in effecting a rescue. That was the occasion that won for Guynemer the rank of lieutenant, and the decoration of the *croix de guerre*.

Let us read one of the brief entries in his diary,

61

for January 26, 1917. He has been attacking a Boche plane in his best manner by descending on it from above, when his gun becomes disabled.

I try to bluff. I mount to 2000 feet over him and drop onto him like a stone. For a moment I think that was without effect when he begins to descend. I put myself ten yards behind him, but every time I showed my nose around the edge of his tail the gunner took aim at me.

We take the road towards Compeigne—3000 feet—2000 feet —again I show my nose and this time the gunner lets go his machine gun and motions to me that he surrenders. *All right!*

I see four bombs stowed away under his machine. 1500 feet. The Boche slows down his windmill. I swerve over him while he lands, but not having any gun or ammunition I cannot prevent the Boches from setting fire to their taxi, a 200 H. P. Albatros, magnificent. When I see that they are safely surrounded I come down and show the Boches my crippled machine gun.

If it seemed to others that he ran needless risks in the spirit of untamed adventure, he always declared that he never took random chances—that he saw his way. His extraordinary quickness of eye and movement, together with his absolute fearlessness that saved him from indecision at a critical moment, account for many of his seemingly miraculous escapes. His individual method of acting both as pilot and gunner was another source of strength; it enabled him to carry more gasoline and ammunition, and his aim was as sure as his management of his wings. The gun, which was attached to the top of the machine over his head, was controlled by a lever that could be operated with one hand. The sights were directly in front so that he aimed by pointing his machine.

Guynemer, the practical machinist, was, moreover, always on duty before every flight. No one could accuse him of recklessness and say that he was saved through some magic of luck who saw him prepare for an attack. He spent an hour in carefully, lovingly, examining his aëroplane and gun. Every screw and buckle was put to the test. Every cartridge was inspected and oiled, together with all the other parts of his equipment. He knew the exact condition of his motor and propeller, and so was sure what he could count on in case of stress.

Guynemer's squadron, ''The Storks,'' so called from the flying stork painted on the side of each machine, included more aviators of note than any other escadrille. Fourteen members of this group brought down a third of all the German machines destroyed before January, 1918, two hundred in less than three years, according to the official count.

FIGHTERS FOR PEACE

Among all of the famous "Storks," René Dormé was second only to Guynemer in the management of his machine and the sureness of his aim. His disappearance over the enemy lines after a fierce battle in the clouds four months before the loss of Guynemer himself, was mourned by all his comrades. On the day that he went from them, May 25, 1917, Guynemer scored his famous quadruple victory. It seemed as if the strength born of his avenging rage knew no bounds. Seeing three machines flying together toward the French lines, he made one of his spectacular mounts, swooped down upon them, and put them to flight. Pursuing, he succeeded in getting one in the line of fire and brought it to earth in flames.

The one weakness of Guynemer's solitary method of fighting was the danger of rear attack. That was where his marvellous agility came into play—darting, turning, he seemed ready at every point. After bringing down, now, his first Boche, the avenger wheeled and saw a second trying to reach him at the moment he was intent upon his conquest; but he had already received from above one of the French explosive bullets, and in a moment fell in flames like his companion. A third Boche who dared to approach the French aviation

THE LATE CAPTAIN GEORGES GUYNEMER
French Ace

field at noon of the same day was sighted by Guynemer, who was at the time high in the air.
Swooping down like a wrathful spirit, he fired
but one shot when the rash enemy fell to earth;
the bullet had found the head of the pilot. That
same evening Guynemer mounted again and
brought down his fourth machine in flames—a
spectacular finish for his great day.

It was this quadruple victory that won for Guynemer the Rosette of the Legion of Honor which
was presented with this commendation:

"An elite officer, a fighting pilot as skilful as audacious.
He has rendered glowing service to his country, both by the
number of his victories and the daily example he has set of
burning ardor and even greater mastery increasing from day
to day. Unconscious of danger, on account of his sureness
of method and precision of maneuvers, he has become the most
redoubtable of all to the enemy. On May 25, 1917, he accomplished one of his most brilliant exploits, beating down two
enemy airplanes in one minute, and gaining two more victories
the same day. By all of his exploits he has contributed towards exalting the courage and enthusiasm of those, who, from
the trenches, were the witnesses of his triumphs. He has
brought down forty-five airplanes, received twenty citations
and been seriously wounded twice."

But I think that more than any eulogy of the
great or adoration of the crowd, Georges Guynemer would have held dear this fervid tribute of
little Franc-Comtois Paul Bailly, an eleven-year-

old schoolboy in the village of Bouclans, who was selected by his mates to speak for them in a composition written on the day set apart for the commemoration of the life of the hero of aces in the schools:

> Guynemer is the Roland of our epoch. Like Roland he was very valiant, and like Roland, he died for France. But his exploits are not a legend, like those of Roland; they are more splendid when told in simple truth than if they had been invented. For his glorification there is to be written in the Pantheon his own among the other great names. His aeroplane is placed in the Invalides. At our school a day is consecrated to him; we have his portrait on our wall; we have learned his last citation in the army orders as a lesson; we have traced his name for penmanship; and we have made a drawing of an aeroplane.
>
> Roland was the pattern of the chevaliers of another age. Guynemer becomes the pattern of the French of to-day and all will try to follow his example. I indeed shall never forget him; I shall keep the remembrance that he, like my dear papa, died for France.

And so it was that to young and old, to the soldiers in the trenches, to workmen in the factories, and to war-weary people throughout the land, Guynemer was the incarnation of the glorious, unconquerable soul of France.

In the summer of 1917, the young hero's friends sought to prevail upon him to take some much-needed rest.

"You wanted to bring down fifty; that was the goal that you set for yourself. Can you not now be satisfied for a little?" pleaded his father.

"They will think I have stopped because I have won all the honors they have to give; they will think that I fought for the prizes!" said Georges. "It is my life to fly."

"But surely now that you are the leader of the squadron you must see that you have enough work for a while in planning, in teaching and directing us all," urged his companions.

"How can you expect me to hold back and hoard myself when adventure beckons?" he replied. "Bringing down Boches is meat and drink to me."

Guynemer loved his little machine with clipped wings as Roland did his horse. Though he won his aceship in a slower model, his favorite steed could rise 10,000 feet in ten minutes and maintain the rate of 120 miles an hour. This "scorner of the ground" lost its buoyancy when the speed was less than 60 miles, and it was, therefore, necessary to bring it to a landing at that rate. How Guynemer chafed when, in the stress of a moment, he was forced to use a borrowed machine. Now his own model is kept, a sacred relic, in the Invalides.

FIGHTERS FOR PEACE

In one of the old hero tales of the Norse we read that when the gods wished to summon Sigmund, the glorious, to the joys of Valhalla, Odin, himself, stayed his hand in the midst of battle, and broke his magic sword. We might believe that the Chevalier of Flight was singled out by the gods that August, for his marvellous power seemed all at once to pass from him. He struggled fiercely against fate—in one day flying seven hours and engaging in several encounters, but all without a single success. On September 10, the day before the last flight, he attempted to set out in three different machines, but all proved contrary and forced him back to earth. That evening his companions, despairing of making him listen to reason, telephoned to his old commanding officer to come and carry him off before he did himself a mischief. Commander Brocard wired Guynemer that he was coming to see him at nine o'clock the next morning.

It seemed as if the young eagle divined their schemes to cage him. At eight o'clock, calling Lieutenant Bozon-Verduras to accompany him, Guynemer set out on his last flight. As in the case of the greatest heroes, his passing was shrouded in mystery. The French peasants declare that he was never brought to the ground, but that his dauntless wings carried him straight up to heaven. All that his companion could tell was this: Guynemer sighted an enemy machine and flew to the attack, leaving him to ward off a possible interference from a group of fighting planes in the distance. They turned off in another direction, however, without seeing the eagle circling above. When the lieutenant returned to his station, the eagle had passed out of sight. "Surely," he thought, "he brought down his game and followed to see the finish."

But that was the last that was seen of the leader of the "Storks."

News of his disappearance was carefully suppressed, so that his chances of escape might not be lessened in case he had been forced to land in enemy territory. But in spite of everything, a London newspaper of September 17 gave out the story of his loss, and some days after this the Cologne "Gazette" printed an item, saying casually that a pilot to fame unknown, one Wisseman, had written home that he had brought down, *on September 10,* the great ace of aces, and so could not doubt his power to conquer everywhere! Though the Germans had always been accustomed

69

to announce immediately the fall of an enemy aviator, this was the only news of the great Guynemer that was forthcoming for ten days after his disappearance.

Application was made through the Red Cross to Germany for official information as to the disposition of his body, and the reply came that after he had been brought down *on September 10* he was buried with military honors in the cemetery at Poelcappelle in Belgium. When this village a few days later fell into the hands of the British, however, the search for his grave was in vain. In reply to a further request for information, the news was vouchsafed that Guynemer's body could not be removed from the wreck of his machine because of the unceasing artillery fire, which finally, in flames and upturned earth destroyed every trace of the aeroplane and its pilot.

It may be that the children and the untaught peasants are right when they say that the life of the marvellous boy ended in a miracle. At any rate his fiery spirit left no cold ashes to be returned to Mother Earth, even to the sacred soil of his beloved France, when it passed into the eternal sky—fire unto fire!

THE CHEVALIER OF FLIGHT

On the tablet erected to his memory in the Pantheon are inscribed these words:

"Captain Guynemer, commander of Squadron No. 3, died on the field of honor September 11, 1917. A hero of legendary power, he fell in the wide heaven of glory, after three years of hard fighting. He will long remain the purest symbol of the qualities of the race: indomitable in tenacity, enthusiastic in energy, sublime in courage. Animated with inextinguishable faith in victory, he bequeaths to the French soldier the imperishable remembrance which will exalt the spirit of sacrifice and the most noble emulation."

"LE PATRON":
(The Boss)

MARSHAL FOCH

"Victory is a thing of the will. . . . A lost battle is a battle one believes oneself to have lost. A battle, then, can only be lost morally, and it is only morally that a battle is won."

MARSHAL FOCH.

"LE PATRON"
(The Boss)

WHAT manner of man is Marshal Foch, the man who brought the one thing needful for the success of the Allied Forces—unity? For, as all of their early defeats were due to the lack of a man big enough to bring together all the diverse elements and varying national ideals and ambitions that fought side by side in the great Army of Freedom, so the last splendid victories were directly due to the presence of that "foursquare man"—the sort of balanced character, that, the great Napoleon declared, the successful leader must be. For while, like the Little Corporal, he is small of stature, (as if Fate wished to prove that human power depends not upon material factors but upon "divine" elements) the man whom the French soldiers call *le patron,* the Boss, and the great generals of all the Allied Armies have hailed as Generalissimo, is not only, quoting Joffre, "the greatest strategist in Europe and the humblest,'' but one of the greatest military commanders of all time.

The measure of the man is indicated in his famous message sent to Joffre at the crisis of the first battle of the Marne:

"My right has been rolled up; my left has been driven in;—consequently, with all that I have left in my centre, I now will attack!"

So it was that in the very midst of disaster, he never allowed himself for a moment to think defeat. For with all his soul Foch believes "A lost battle is a battle one believes oneself to have lost; in a material sense no battle can be lost. A battle, then, can only be lost morally, and it is only morally that a battle is won." Never for an instant did Foch swerve from his faith in the ultimate victory. His first quoted utterance after assuming the supreme command was typical of his attitude: "The future will show the full measure of our success. All is going well."

But if this finely tempered optimism, that is much more than a matter of sanguine temperament, having its roots in his sober, reasoned philosophy of life, accounts in a measure for his success, it is yet only half the story. He has shown first and last a determined bulldog tenacity that may be compared to General Grant's *I shall fight it out on this line if it takes all summer.* Another incident that has become part of the history of the first battle of the Marne will illustrate this characteristic, which was, in the balanced character of the leader, what reserves are in the constitution of an army. At the height of the struggle when Foch was carrying out his superb counter-offensive in the presence of apparent failure, one of his officers rode up to him and said, "It is impossible to persist further; my men are tired out."

"Tired out!" exclaimed Foch sharply; "so are the Germans! Attack!"

Thus, in the account of Foch's part in bringing about "the miracle of the Marne," we have the keynote of his character.

Everybody felt that the Battle of the Marne was a veritable miracle, but still everybody wanted to know what the chief human factor was in bringing about the victory that shattered Von Bülow's army, checkmated Von Kluck, and saved Paris.

"There are just two things that you can pick out," said a French officer. "The first was the way in which Joffre hurled Manoury's army on the flank of Von Kluck, bringing him once for all to a halt; the other—and I am inclined to think it as great a factor—was the wonderful strategy of Foch. At a moment when he seemed too weak to maintain the defensive, he saved himself and won the day by a brilliant counter-attack. Discovering a gap between two German armies, he directed his batteries at that point with such telling effect that a veritable panic took possession of the lines raked by our 75's. This success was planned to occupy the enemy and screen his master-stroke—a surprise maneuver similar to that of Joffre's. Seizing a neighboring division on the left, he swept it around to the right in a sudden pounce on the German flank.''

In one of Foch's celebrated books on the science of war, we find some bits of interesting philosophy. ''Victory is a thing of the will,'' he says; and ''A general must possess the energy to take the necessary risks.'' His own career gives admirable point to his teaching, for, rooted and grounded in his certain faith in the ultimate victory, his *will to win* was indeed invincible, and he saw that the necessary risks were so many God-given opportunities, to be seized with an energy that would never fail so long as it refused to entertain the thought of defeat.

"LE PATRON"

Foch knew that pessimism is a confession of weakness, so he watched for indications of depression in the enemy as he watched for weak points in their lines.

"War is not an exact science, it is a terrifying and passionate drama!" he used to say. In his strategy, then, he took account of the mind and moral attitude of the enemy. "We must maneuver if we are going to bring to bear a superior force at a certain point," he said, "and we get the full effect of the surprise by the sudden appearance of danger which the enemy cannot ward off. Never let yourself look upon a battle as a mere artillery duel. It is a struggle of moral forces and morale will win."

Once again, who is this great strategist who is also a psychologist and a philosopher? What is the personality behind the power?

Ferdinand Foch was born October 2, 1851, in the town of Tarbes in the foot-hills of the Pyrenees. It is a curious coincidence that his birthplace was only four miles distant from that of Joffre, and that the two Marne generals were within a few months of the same age. Both were brilliant mathematicians and both were artillerymen. Both had their first taste of war at the siege

79

of Paris in 1871. Both had somewhat similar colonial experience in Madagascar. But there the parallel ends. Joffre, big, patient and solid, was by temperament a cautious, defensive fighter; Foch, something below medium, slight and quick, was in theory and practice a believer in maintaining the offensive even out of apparent weakness.

Some have declared that the Foch family has an Alsatian strain, which accounts for the suspiciously Teutonic look of the name. (It is pronounced as if it were spelled Foche, the o very long.) But he is in fact much nearer being a Spaniard, for there is a dash of Basque blood in his veins, and his early childhood was spent within sight of the hills of Spain. There was nothing, however, of the dreamer of castles in Spain in the child Ferdinand or in the youth who was distinguished for his proficiency in geometry and logic. He loved the exact sciences, turning away instinctively from the vague and intangible.

"His feet are always planted firmly on the ground, and his head is always level," said one of his students at the Ecole de Guerre—France's famous war college—"but he is not one who thinks that you can bring a yardstick to the judgment of all the facts of the universe.''

Does it seem a matter of surprise that the first strategist in Europe was once an instructor who was so enthusiastic in his work and so inspiring in his influence that he was called a ''born teacher''? He taught more than the bare facts; he developed the power to think, and his strong personality commanded respect and quickened character.

''The officers who passed through the Ecole de Guerre between 1896 and 1907 will never lose the impression produced on them by their professor of strategy and tactics. The course was eagerly looked forward to as the fundamental teaching of the school,'' said one of his former pupils. ''When directing a skeleton or map maneuver, he put his officers through a veritable course of intellectual gymnastics. It was impossible to circumvent him by approximations or compromises; he always held you up with his famous: 'Now what is the point?' He was an excellent teacher because he had a passion for teaching.''

The philosophy of General Foch, which profoundly influenced his work as a teacher, as we see in his published volumes of lectures, "The Principles of War" and "Concerning the Waging of War," had its source in deep religious convictions. The faith that he was taught in his childhood grew and ripened with the experiences of the years. Never a thing apart, it was the unifying principle of his practical conceptions of life. "He is the only man of theory I ever knew who was better in practice," said an English officer.

"Do you recall that I come of a religious family, to whom the church is of tremendous moment?" said Foch one day to Premier Clemenceau, who had just informed him, over their after-luncheon coffee and cigars, that he had been appointed Director of the Ecole de Guerre. "What will the politicians say to your putting up a man whose brother is a Jesuit priest? Why, I have not even been a candidate!"

"That is just it!" replied the "Tiger." "This is one classic instance of the office seeking the man. Besides I think you have the added distinction of being the one eligible officer who has n't been a candidate."

"But you have n't taken into account the frightful handicap of my religion," put in Foch again, the suspicion of a twinkle in his eyes.

"LE PATRON"

"Well, General," returned the "Tiger," "not all the Jesuits in the world or all the suspicions of the anti-church party can together keep you from taking the job you're the man for!"

And so, first as teacher of military history and theory and later as Commandant, Foch exerted a powerful, determining influence upon the classes of young officers who directed the French divisions in the Great War. In a very real sense, therefore, the French army is Foch's army, from the men in the ranks, who, to the last *poilu* of them all, rely implicitly upon *le patron,* to the colonels and commanders who were imbued through and through with a single ideal: France must profit by the hard lesson of the defeat of 1871. Sure of herself and her cause, she must have the courage to dominate events—to seize and keep the offensive at all costs.

"What a confession of weakness it was," said a French captain, "when the Germans gave up open fighting and took to the trenches. They could do nothing more than prolong the struggle and delay the inevitable end in that way. Moreover, time was fighting for us, since Germany was in effect a besieged city. But only a nation with a cause and a sure faith could have kept on with the aggressive part after a defeat like that of the Marne.''

General Foch's faith in victory was not of the sort that refuses to face the difficulties to be surmounted. We are told that when he was questioned during the dark days of 1914, for his judgment in regard to the struggle, he used to reply in three short words: *"Long, dûr, sûr."* (Long, hard, sure.) And the four years that succeeded proved that he was a true prophet.

The way in which Foch kept ahead of the Germans in the famous "race to the sea" well illustrates what force there was behind those three words as uttered by the master strategist, who also declared with a conviction that could only come from practical experience, "No man need ever be tired in a crisis if he manages his mind right."

Picture the situation when the Germans, after the Marne check, were trying to pass on through Western France and outflank the French army. Seeing the danger, the French kept extending their lines westward to bar the way. Thus the two armies were, in effect, racing to the coast, which, when reached, would put an end to any further move to get behind and envelop the Allied armies.

"LE PATRON"

The Germans, who had superior numbers and equipment of every sort,—railway material, motor trucks, and every means of transportation, together with their big guns,—seemed to have heavy odds on their side. But there they came against Foch, with his power to seize the vital points of a situation and multiply his force by swift and well-calculated movement. It was as if each man under his skilful strategy did the work of two. Every unit was dynamic at every moment—and Foch always managed to get on the spot first.

Of all the brilliant French leaders, Foch was the one best understood and most warmly admired by the British. This was partly because his temperament accorded happily with the English attitude.

"That little man would be hopeful if he had a bullet through his middle," said Tommy Atkins.

"He lives and flourishes by mental pluck," said a London newspaper correspondent.

It was, however, not only his invigorating optimism which won for him the whole-hearted confidence of the British, but the fact that he was indeed a four-square man—that he did not flinch before the *"long* and *dûr"* of the fighting while he insisted on the *sûr* of the victory. It was really a beautiful thing to see Lloyd George's look of content when he spoke of General Foch's selection as Commander-in-chief. He knew that at last the Allies had a leader who would bring them all together—a man who would meet every stress and rise to every emergency.

That was shown at the first battle of Ypres, when British cooks, orderlies and porters—the last muster of reserves—were trying to hold back the German hordes, battalion on battalion of picked men, and, as it would seem, unlimited reenforcements. At the darkest moment when the British were quite spent and the Belgians all but despairing of holding the line at the Yser, Foch arrived with a sufficient number of reserves and his faith in a determined offensive. As one correspondent put it, "he loosed the dikes and flooded the Germans with Frenchmen." Putting up his trusty 75's in any cover that came to hand, he promptly shattered the Huns' belief in the possibility of a drive. With a greatly inferior force which he kept moving in small but telling counter-attacks, he won the day. Again as at the Marne, he proved the virtue of his swift and well-timed offensive as the surest means of defense.

British officers and historians were unanimous

in lauding Foch as the one to whom they owed
it that Calais and the other Channel ports were not
seized for submarine bases. In token of the nation's gratitude, King George promptly bestowed
on the French commander the Order of the Bath, a
distinction given only to those who have rendered
the greatest service to England.

"Why did you have so few prisoners to show
for your victory at Ypres?" Foch was asked.

"It must have been because our machine guns
and bayonets gave the Boches no chance to think
of surrender," he replied.

It was once said of Foch that he was of the
"Bonaparte and Kaiser kind" in his willingness
to sacrifice lives in order to score in the great
game. "Well," he retorted, when timidly challenged by an American attaché in regard to his
policy, "your own Grant did not believe in spar-
ing men when the need came, did he?"

"That is true," acquiesced the American.
"One must sacrifice to win."

"Don't misunderstand and misquote me now,"
said Foch, a twinkle in his blue-gray eyes. "It
is the Germans I believe in sacrificing; I never
throw away my own soldiers."

"What is the secret of the Boss's uncanny instinct for hitting upon just the right spots for his surprise attacks?'' queried an ambitious American lieutenant who believed in improving the chance that had put him opposite a thoughtful French captain at dinner.

''It would seem as if he not only studies the present condition of the enemy—his material and moral assets—but from that point of departure he studies also the future.'' The Captain paused, choosing his words. ''Of course the roots of the future are in the present; and Foch seems to have power to divine the nature and trend of the growth from what now exists. He puts himself face to face with the enemy's problems, sees the way he'll try to meet them, and then with that grip on the future, our General makes it his business to strike first. There is every advantage in that first blow. And, you must admit,'' he added with a laugh, ''that, when it is a matter of being quick and on the spot the Hun with his ponderous Kultur is no match for a Frenchman.''

Would you like to get a glimpse of the Foch that the members of his staff know? The Paris ''L'Illustration'' pictures his headquarters at the rear of the lines where, in a room without chairs since everybody there is always at alert attention,

MARSHAL FERDINAND FOCH
Commander-in-Chief of the Allied Forces

the General stands before a map of the fighting area as if he were in a classroom. About him are grouped in the strictest military fashion a number of officers—the members of his staff.

The "Boss" has direct blue-gray eyes, set wide apart under a high forehead; the nose is large and finely cut, the chin powerful. One is immediately impressed by the serenity and also by the nervous energy of his face. He stands motionless, except that now and then he tugs abruptly at his iron-gray moustache. His even tones carry authority and conviction. . . . An officer enters, salutes, and makes a report. Foch looks intently at the map, draws a line, puts a question, and then turns back to the map as the officer takes a place among the rest of the staff. He is, like Joffre, a man of few words when at the post of command.

As Generalissimo, he is the one who decides for all the armies of the Allies the points for attack and those for withdrawal; the immediate placing of the army of maneuver; and the exact moment for passing from the defense to aggression. Under his direction, not only the forces on the Western front—six million men of eight different nationalities—acted together as one mighty army; but also the armies in Palestine, in Bulgaria, and in Italy, timed their moves as parts of the great whole.

"You officers who simply know the General at headquarters, have never seen the real man," said one of his friends. "It is only when he is out of doors that *le Patron* relaxes his hold and gives the man a chance—the man who loves the woods, who knows the trees as intimates of his spirit. And he is almost as much at his ease among books and pictures as he is in the saddle."

His hours with his horse, *Croesus,* a splendid chestnut, who was his favorite companion through all the campaigns of the war, gave the General the rest and renewal he most needed while he was carrying the plans of the world battles in his mind and heart. Like Napoleon, he found that a brisk canter could, on occasion, take the place of hours of sleep.

It is the time of the great German offensive, launched March 21, 1918, which held the centre of the world stage until the middle of April. Foch is biding his time, upheld by his faith in the victory and a patience like that of Joffre. He is holding all his forces in leash, even when he sees the Allied line broken and his armies in retreat. His confidence seems born of a power to judge aright the factors that are working against him in the present moment and to see what the future has in store. He reads as in an open book the conditions underlying this desperate spending of every resource in man power and munitions. It is a gambler's mad stake on one last throw.

Calmly he waits, letting the enemy spend himself. The Germans reason that he is overwhelmed by the mighty onslaught, that their advance has crushed all power of resistance. Why need to worry about food supplies? Hindenburg assures the people at home that by the first of May they will be in Paris and have the Allies at their mercy.

Still Foch bides his time. He knows that this wave of success must soon break; he knows that the situation must indeed be desperate when a great leader pins all his faith on one stroke, making no preparation for a blow at any other point. It must be a race with starvation. Once again the Germans prove their inability to gauge either the resources or the morale of the nations ranged against them. They see in Foch's waiting only a confession of weakness, and their assurance grows. Recklessly they plunge on. The Allied line gives way before them reluctantly, but it yields, even as far as the Marne.

There, out of breath as it were, the Germans pause a moment. Since every offensive with its concentrated effort leads to a shrinking of the lines, there comes inevitably a point where a lull is necessary in order to give room for maneuver. Then a general must be ready to strike at another point if he does not want to lose the initiative. But when, in April, the German offensive wore itself out at the Marne, Foch knew that his hour had come. They should see that they had to reckon with a force that would not allow them to take their good time to recover. The chance of following up their victory would never come.

There were two alternatives before Foch. He might attempt a strong blow on the German flank, or he might try a succession of blows at several points. There is always a temptation to try for the big thing—for the one decisive stroke for which everybody longs. But Foch saw that the enemy had still great striking power and that they were at their best between Rheims and the North Sea where their excellent system of communication would make the shifting of forces from point to point easy. He decided on a hammering policy that aimed to reduce their numbers and their morale bit by bit. It was as if he said to himself: "I will give them chance to experience nothing but blow upon blow until they get in the habit of thinking defeat."

What uncanny power gave the master strategist his instinct for the exact point to strike? Always he selected a spot where the Germans were trying to effect a retirement or one from which they were attempting to bring reserves. As soon as the exasperated Von Ludendorf, (who had succeeded Hindenburg as chief of staff) tried to shift a few battalions from another section to relieve the one under stress, along came another irritating check right at that point! It was really most annoying to be delayed by such petty engagements when he was almost ready to set in motion a drive so colossal that the Kaiser's enemies should be forever confounded.

But Foch continued to hammer away, now with the army of Byng at Cambrai; now with the forces of Rawlinson at St. Quentin. Again, the storm centre shifted to St. Mihiel or the Meuse, where Pershing's men rose to the attack. Then, at the very moment an attempt was made to abandon the territory between Ypres and the sea, the English, French and Belgians fell upon the retreating columns and forced them willy-nilly into line.

They were not allowed to shorten their front and retire rapidly to a carefully prepared position that might give them a better fighting chance. Instead of being merely driven back, they were compelled to stand and take blow after blow.

It must have been a terrifying and tragic moment when it finally dawned upon Ludendorf and his henchmen that they had been out-generaled, and that the end could only be a question of weeks. The Germans could see too that Foch was able to pursue his relentless strategy without check because of two blunders of their own: First, the terrible waste of men in their glorious spring drive; second, the coming of the despised American troops, which had shifted the balance of manpower to the side of the Allies.

With every day the condition of the enemy became more desperate. The soldiers who were seeing their lines struck everywhere felt the helplessness of their leaders and began to "think defeat." Many allowed themselves to be taken after only a half-hearted attempt at defense. The hammering method does not produce panic; it reduces morale and power.

On October 8, when Foch threw three British armies against the line between Cambrai and St.

Quentin, it was plain that the end was in sight. Five weeks later Germany had entirely collapsed, her armies driven from their defenses—Hindenburg's wonderful series of "lines," which, like the water-tight compartments of a boat, were designed to give security during storm after storm of attack.

Then came the great day when the representatives of the German people waited upon Marshal Foch at his headquarters to receive from him the terms upon which they might have an armistice. The master strategist who had led the foe to the point of defeat was the man who bade them sign the paper of surrender.

General Foch has received many honors from his own country and from the Allies. As victor of the second battle of the Marne, he was, like Joffre, presented with the baton of a Marshal of France. When the end came there was no higher reward to bestow. But surely the man who held that "victory is a thing of the will," and that "it is only morally that a battle can be won," must have felt in that unconditional surrender of his country's foe his true reward. The *will to win* had triumphed.

THE "TIGER" AS MAN OF VICTORY

PREMIER CLEMENCEAU

"We, women of France, mothers, wives, sisters of the brave soldiers of Normandy . . . to you, tireless fighter, champion of justice, Frenchman and patriot, we appeal. We rally under your flag, the emblem of energy; we have faith in your standard."

Petition of French Women to Clemenceau.

THE "TIGER" AS MAN OF VICTORY

THERE was a man who earned the name of "Tiger" from his fellow countrymen, because, it was said, he had "torn, clawed and bitten his way into power." He had attacked and overthrown so many public servants of high office that he was called "Destroyer of Ministries," and "The Stormy Petrel of French Politics." Of all men he was easily first in the gentle art of making enemies. Yet it came to pass that in the time of her direst need, when France feared that treachery or weakness at home might bring defeat to her heroic armies at the front, when people said, "We must have a man whom all can without the shadow of a doubt trust to lead us through this war," the country turned with one accord to that destructive force, and said: "Clemenceau must be our Premier! We know that he will make our government safe for victory!"

How did it happen that the destroyer came to be hailed as the preserver? That is the story of the career of the Tiger of France.

FIGHTERS FOR PEACE

Georges Clemenceau was born September 28, 1841, in a little village of Brittany. His father, a physician who cared more to give his skill to the poor than to work for the fees of the rich, was an ardent Republican whose days were embittered by seeing his country fall into the clutches of "Napoleon the Little," as Victor Hugo styled the upstart ruler of the Second Empire. He loved truth and fair dealing; he also loved the fair face of Nature—the changes and surprises of sunlight and shadow among the trees, upon the water. In his leisure moments when he was not pondering over some weighty problem concerning the government of France or of the Universe, he was trying to catch with his palette of colors a bit of the beauty that gladdened his eyes.

The intense soul of this father, who hated tyranny and shams no less fiercely than he loved the simple human heritage of quiet work and happy play of mind and heart, lighted kindred fires in the spirit of his son. When the lad was ten years of age his nature was stirred to the depths by seeing his wise, kindly father led away, handcuffed, to prison. He had dared to protest against the *coup d'état* by which at one stroke the President, Louis

Napoleon, was exalted to the dizzy throne of Emperor of France.

The boy threw his arms about his father, whispering, "Some day I will avenge you, *mon père*."

"If you want to really accomplish that, you will have to work, you know," said the father, who could not return the embrace of his son save by a long look, as searching as it was tender. "Nothing comes of itself in this world; toil brings the harvests."

The father could not, however, by his most searching look discover anything particularly promising in this son. He was not a good student; at the age of sixteen he knew little more than many lads of twelve. For only one subject had he shown real enthusiasm, and that was for the study of English.

"Why do you care more for English than for other things?" he was asked.

"Because I want to read 'Robinson Crusoe'—all of it, just as it is—for myself," was the amazing reply.

Then, at seventeen, the boy had a sudden awakening. It seemed as if all at once the windows of his mind were thrown open, and the sunshine of a

world of interests came flooding in to warm and
quicken him. He began to read everything
eagerly, hungrily. The days were not long enough
for all the splendid possibilities. If it is true that
life is measured by one's points of contact with his
environment, then young Clemenceau was very
much alive, for there was no corner of existence
without its interest for him.

It is not surprising that at nineteen he should
have decided without question that he was to be
a doctor. How could he do better than to follow
in the footsteps of his large-hearted, keen-minded
father? The study of medicine, therefore, did not
fill his days to the exclusion of all else. There
was time for books and friends; there was time for
strolls about Paris, and, on a Sunday morning,
for real wanderings out beyond the streets into
the open country. "The thoughts of youth are
long, long thoughts," and Georges Clemenceau's
were given direction by the strong convictions of
his "Jacobin" father.

Perhaps he thought that the hour had come for
him to defy the rule of kings, avenging his father
and all other lovers of liberty. At any rate the
little paper which he brought out with the help of
Emile Zola and another radical companion was

called "Le Travail" (Work). Did he perhaps recall that his father had said on one memorable occasion that work alone could avenge him and further his cause? It would seem that this little sheet was not such a trifling "work" that it could be ignored, for it landed the three young champions of human rights in prison. After a brief sojourn behind bars, this energetic disciple of medicine for the human body and democracy for the body politic, once more called down on his rash head the wrath of the imperial police by shouting "*Vive la Republique!*" from a point of vantage on an avenue of Paris when the gay city was celebrating one of the anniversaries of the fête-loving Second Empire.

"If you care so much for a republic that you don't know when to hold your peace you might go to America—the air and the ideas there may be more to your liking," he was told meaningly.

In brief, young Clemenceau found himself an exile, but instead of repining he seized the opportunity to make a study of the social institutions of Great Britain and the United States. He took with him to America his degree in medicine, some letters to Horace Greeley, and an alert interest in the conditions resulting from the Civil

War. "My first impression of Americans," he said, "is that they have excellent particular convictions, but no general ideas and no good coffee."

Settling first in New York in 1865, he put out his doctor's shingle, and while waiting for a chance to practice, wrote for "Le Temps" a series of articles at once brisk and thoughtful, describing phases of the social and political life in America.

"I used to spend more time in the Astor Library than in my professional habitat on West Twelfth Street, where it was neither pleasant nor profitable to merely wait for patients—the virtue of patience is one for which I have never been particularly noted," said M. Clemenceau, his dark eyes lighting up with a smile which showed that he took some pleasure in his English pun. He became, indeed, remarkably proficient in the language, which he handled in the American fashion, and really well acquainted with American institutions and ideals.

There was one institution—a young ladies' seminary at Stamford, Connecticut—in which he took an especial interest for more than one reason. It meant for him first—what he needed sorely at that time—a certain income. It meant

for the young ladies a series of talks on French
Literature and conversations with a professor who
could be witty and fascinating in two languages.
It meant for the canny schoolmistress an opportunity for agreeable economy, since the French instructor was also a proficient riding master.
"Imagine the Tiger of France cantering across
country with a bevy of charming American
mademoiselles, just out of school for a holiday
afternoon. That was certainly a time when one
might have seen a smile on the face of the Tiger!"
said an appreciative Frenchman. We may con-
clude that the young professor was not wanting in
appreciation, for when he returned to France in
1870 he took with him an American bride—one
of the fair pupils from the seminary.

The most spirited dialogues in class or on horseback could hardly have prepared young Madame
Clemenceau for the France to which she was introduced. Those were tense, stirring times that
Paris knew at the close of the war with Prussia,
and Clemenceau, who had settled in the feverishly
radical district of Montmartre, was from the first
in the midst of the excitement. A former comrade, who now was a member of the Government of
National Defense, promptly nominated the re-

turned exile mayor of Montmartre, and he at once
proved himself in the turmoil of public affairs one
to the manner born. He had strong convictions,
and a sincerity and power in presenting them that
carried conviction to others.

"One felt that he had thought things out—he
knew where he stood and why. Besides he cared
enough about a matter and had resolution enough,
to stand his ground no matter what came or went.
It was that strength of purpose that made him a
power in politics," it was said.

In 1871, he was chosen member of the National
Assembly by 96,000 votes. The son of the
"Jacobin" physician of Brittany had shown that
he could work, and fight too, for the cause of the
people. He was distinctly the man of the hour
in the camp of the radicals.

Something occurred at this time which stirred
the people's candidate more profoundly than had
anything since the day when he saw his father led
away to prison. He saw his beloved country bereft
of two of her fairest daughter-provinces—Alsace
and Lorraine. Bitterly, desperately, he opposed
the treaty that gave this sacred soil of France into
the keeping of the enemy. It seemed that the
patriotic soul of Georges Clemenceau received its

baptism in the fiery trial of that time. His love for France became the great passion of his life.

Years afterward, Clemenceau, the Premier-pilot of the good ship, "Victory," tried to tell about a moment when those who had suffered greatly through the war were moved by the mighty love of country out of themselves—beyond the thought of their sorrows and hardships. "There they were—" he said, "men, hats off, motionless as statues, proud of becoming great through their children. Mothers, with seared faces, superbly stoic under the eye of the greater maternity of the great country. The children in the ecstasy of feeling about them something greater than they can understand, but already certain that they will understand some day this immortal hour. And not a cry, not a word sounds in the air, nothing but the great silence of the courage of all of them. Then every one goes away, firm and erect, to a glorious destiny. In every heart La France has passed." Do we not divine in the intense feeling of these words something of the ardent patriotism that thrilled every fibre of his being? In his heart, too, La France had passed.

Only a faithful lover of country and a stanch champion of democracy could have kept his ideals

of both undimmed and undiminished during the
period that followed the downfall of the Second
Empire and the siege of Paris. As the excesses
of the Reign of Terror had succeeded the reign of
the Bourbons, so the bloody Commune avenged
the extravagances and follies of Napoleon III.
Clemenceau's district of Montmartre was the
very storm centre of mob violence and terrorism.
Thither, the French President, Thiers, who had
been chosen head of the restored Republic, dis-
patched some troops of the regular army under
the Generals Lecomte and Clement-Thomas. In
the wild riot that ensued the two commanders were
shot. Political opponents of M. Clemenceau, who
feared his growing influence, at once seized upon
this tragedy to bring about his downfall. For once
the radical leader deigned to speak at length in his
own defense:

"They accused me of being an accomplice in the
murder of the Generals—a deliberate falsehood,"
he declared with flashing eyes. "This is what
really happened. Two hundred prisoners, whom
I had to protect against popular fury, were confined in the town-hall the day of the murder of
the Generals. I could know nothing of what was
going on outside. I heard in a neighboring square

gay music accompanying the tramp of marching troops. I believed that General Thomas was safely out of France and I knew that General Lecomte was a prisoner at Chateaurouge, but under the care of brave and determined men. About three o'clock in the afternoon a captain came running up and told me that the two generals had been led to a neighboring house and were in great and imminent danger. My duty was to rush to their assistance; but who would take care of my prisoners! There happened to be in my office one of my young friends, a student; to him I delegated my powers and made him *per interim* Mayor of Montmartre and hurried out, followed by the Captain. However, some one stopped me and said: 'There is no need of going further. You are too late. All is done.' Around me I saw looks of hatred; I heard angry cries and shouts of 'Treason! Treason!' They believed that I was following the bloody policy of M. Thiers. I was carried along, buffeted by the crowd, threatened with fists and revolvers, and it took me an hour to retrace my ten-minute walk from the *Mairie*."

Nevertheless Clemenceau kept his faith in the free rule of a free people, though he believed that growth could only come through strenuous endeavor and struggle. It was as if the words he had heard when a boy "Nothing comes of itself in this world; toil brings the harvests," found an echo in the convictions of the man. "There is no rest for free peoples," he said. "Rest is a monarchic idea. The people know no rest. If French democracy is ripe for self-government it will no longer know rest nor the peace of silence."

Clemenceau, who was chosen President of the Municipal Council in 1875, and in the following year elected member of the Chamber of Deputies, was from that time forward the determined and fearless leader of the most advanced party of the French Government.

Since he was a servant of the people and of his country, he tried to keep the public in touch with what concerned them and the honor and glory of France. His papers "La Justice," "L'Aurore" and later "L'Homme Libre" were read for the keen, direct criticisms and interpretations of the vital issues of the moment given in his leading editorials. We may say that his influence through his speeches and debates, and with the wider public who hung upon his printed words, was due to the clear-cut, positive character of all he said. He never hedged, qualified, nor veiled his statements with half-negations.

"He isn't planning to change his position to-morrow," people said. "He's an honest man, if a hard one. We can be sure of one politician who puts love of country before gain; he doesn't care how many enemies he makes if he can bring to pass the right thing."

His opponents called him a "parliamentary swashbuckler, without principles and without prejudices." But he kept on, serenely secure in the faith that, while petty politicians have their little day and "there is no rest for free peoples," still democracy is safe since it is impossible to delude all the people all the time.

To one of his ardent champions who protested against a particularly bitter attack upon the honesty of his chief, M. Clemenceau said:

"My young friend, when one has heard for many years under his windows the cry *'Demandez le suicide de M. Clemenceau!'* there must be in life certain things which leave one perfectly indifferent."

He had faith that honest purpose would prove itself and that deeds would speak when words were

111

forgotten. His impatience with speech-making when the time had come for action is shown in the address of classic brevity with which he opened the Allied Conference at Paris:

"Gentlemen, we are here to work. Let us work."

Was it because Clemenceau was determined to prove that "there is no rest for free peoples" by keeping things continually at fever heat, that he attacked the victims of his censure without fear or mercy and won the name of "the Tiger"? The people came to feel that it was because he loved France better than any consideration of self-interest, and that he dared everything in her service. They said: "It is always something that is wrong or weak or stupid that he attacks—something that another man less keen or zealous would shrug his shoulders over and let pass. Clemenceau, the tiger of politicians, is the watch-dog of France!"

Men, wise in the weather signs of political possibilities, said: "Clemenceau is without doubt the strongest man in public life, but he has made too many enemies to ever come into power."

In 1906, however, he was appointed Minister of the Interior, and in the same year Prime Min-

GEORGES CLEMENCEAU
Premier of France

ister. For a moment his enemies were silenced, but when he went out of power three years later they exulted confidently: *"That* is the last of the swashbuckler!"

But it came to pass, as we have seen, that at the time of the greatest crisis France had ever known, the call of the people was so strong and so insistent, that President Poincairé, (who had frequently been the subject of attack in the Tiger's editorials) asked M. Clemenceau to once again take the helm as Premier. The call came also directly, pleadingly, from the people. Some of the appeals touched the veteran statesman profoundly; it was a very mild "Tiger" indeed who read the petition of the women of Normandy:

"We, women of France, mothers, wives, sisters of the brave soldiers of Normandy, profoundly indignant at the scandal of the treachery of those who strike our brave loved ones in the back while offering their blood so valiantly to our dear native land,—to you, tireless fighter, champion of justice, Frenchman and patriot, we appeal. We rally under your flag, the emblem of energy; we have faith in your standard."

On the day of November, 1917, when the new Premier—"the best hated statesman of the Republic" and the best trusted—arose to make his statement in the Chamber of Deputies, it seemed as if the country fairly held its breath. "The Tiger" himself was visibly moved. The dark eyes in the yellow-ivory face smouldered with an intenser fire, and it seemed as if one could see the lips under the drooping gray mustache whiten.

"I am almost afraid to think what is expected of me," he said. "But this you know: I am an old man. I have nothing to gain for myself by being where I am. My one thought is for France, bloody in her glory. What are my war aims, you ask. I have only one—*to win!*"

The people were electrified. The passion of intense purpose that quivered in his face, in his voice, stirred their hearts and strengthened the will to win. Victory seemed near.

France, "bloody in her glory," held her head high, facing the future with confidence. The energy and optimism of the man at the helm had heartened all of the people at a time when enemies abroad and traitors at home had sown the tares of "defeatism" on every hand.

One wondered perhaps now and again if the former leader of the opposition, who had protested against the press censorship in political matters by changing the name of his paper "L'Homme Libre" (The Free Man) to "L'Homme Enchainé" (The Man in Irons), might have liked a little freedom from instant comment and criticism now that he was at the post of command. The paper founded and made famous by him was once more appearing under the name "L'Homme Libre," and all other publications were free from censorship save in military matters. There were, of course, many who questioned and attacked the measures of the new Premier. Before long, however, his vigorous, fearless policy and his genius for administration brought results that justified the faith of the people and silenced his political enemies.

One of his first acts was to bring to justice Caillaux, (at one time Premier and for several terms Minister of Finance), and other arch-traitors to France who had been tools and accomplices of German agents in spreading propaganda of pessimism and "defeatism," designed to lead France and Italy to make an immediate peace. Evidence that certain men prominent in the world of business and finance had received money from Count von Bernstorff, former German ambassador to Washington, for the subsidizing of newspapers,

115

had been unearthed in America; but two successive Ministers of the Interior failed to take any decisive action. Caillaux and his fellow conspirators had too many friends among the rich and powerful. It was in this stress that the people had turned to Clemenceau, confident in his loyalty to France and his fearless honesty. Caillaux had been, indeed, a former political colleague and closely associated with him in many matters of policy. When Clemenceau was made Premier in 1906 he had selected Caillaux as Minister of Finance. Now he was the one man on whom the country could rely to hunt down this dangerous conspirator, and to stamp out his plots. The "Tiger" was truly the watch-dog of France.

Clemenceau brought to his task as administrator a solid knowledge of statecraft garnered through many years from the time when as a youth he had dreamed of serving the cause of the people. His studies in England and America had given him grasp and perspective. It will be remembered that he had followed closely the drama of politics in the United States during the period of Reconstruction following the Civil War. He recalled frequently many interesting phases of the history of that time, painting a vivid picture of the first meeting of Virginia's negro legislature. All of the trials and changes that marked the course of events during the troublous Third Republic of France had left their impress. Endowed with a remarkably tenacious memory, he seemed to derive his power as a statesman as much from his practical assimilation of the results of experience, which meant vitality and breadth of grasp, as from his unflagging zeal in attacking the various factors of the immediate situation that confronted him.

Chosen in the dark moment of crisis of warring hopes and fears, Clemenceau justified the faith of his countrymen by steering a straight course to a reasonable, fortified optimism and the port of Victory. The "Tiger" was so absolutely the man of the hour that it was hard to even imagine the time when France did not have the assurance of his strong hand at the helm. "He so fits the place and the needs of the country, that it seems as if he has been there always," people said. "The former time is like a half-forgotten nightmare."

I like to picture the Premier among the soldiers. As chairman of the Senate Army Committee and as a journalist he had often gone to the front and mingled freely with the men, who adored him.

As Prime Minister he went even oftener. People marvelled at the inexhaustible energy of the man; for he seemed always at the front and yet never away from Paris. One of the trenches was named *Le Tigre* in his honor, and when his familiar gray, mud-stained motor made its way back to the city there was often tucked away in it some token of a poilu's devotion—a pipe, perhaps, or a walking-stick, lovingly carved by one of "his children."

Frequently the officers remonstrated with him for rashly exposing himself to danger. He even refused to wear a steel helmet until the men about him doffed theirs. Then, protesting and scolding, he consented to protect the head that was guiding the destinies of France.

"As if my bald pate mattered!" he said, looking for a long moment, Hamlet-like, at a heap of the slain. "My old carcass *there?* What an end it would be!"

Always a lover of Nature, the Premier finds rest and renewal of strength in the garden of his Paris home. "He will always be young because his interests are so keen," said one of his friends. "It is impossible to even imagine the indifference that is age creeping upon him. In his make-up the temperament of the artist and the spirit of the scientist are perfectly blended. Feeling and understanding go hand in hand.''

As Clemenceau talks about his flowers, his chickens, Japanese art, or the great moment when General Foch was put in command of the armies, he is interesting and delightful, but when he talks about the soldiers of France he is another man. His piercing eyes become tender; voice and gesture alike betray the depth of his feeling.

He is describing a visit to the trenches: "We go down into the ground," he says, "and there we are protected from the 'marmites' in a dark corridor lit by candles stuck into the mouths of German gas masks. We sit down on anything handy (I even have the favor of a chair), before a board which also serves as the colonel's bed, while arms whose body remains invisible serve us with dishes not to be disdained by a gormand. How did they get there? I cannot undertake to explain that. The walk in the open air, the tragic nature of the place, the joy in land reconquered, no doubt all lend particular spice to the comradeship of these men who forget that they have done great deeds as soon as they have done them.''

They say that the name of the ''Tiger'' cannot

now be properly applied to the Man of Victory. His great constructive work for France, his whole-hearted tenderness for the soldiers—for all who have suffered through the war—have left no room for thought of the tearing and rending of political strife. He no longer seems the embodiment of the France of bitter rivalry and struggle, but of the old France of romance and beauty, the new France of strength and heroism, the undying France of glory and power. He will be remembered not as the "Tiger," but as the lover of France and the Premier of Victory.

THE MAN BEHIND THE GUNS:

DAVID LLOYD GEORGE

There are rare epochs in the history of the world when in a few raging years the character, the destiny of the whole race, is determined for unknown ages. This is one. The winter wheat is being sown. It is better, it is surer, it is more bountiful in its harvest, than when it is sown in the soft spring time. There are many storms to pass through, there are many frosts to endure, before the land brings forth its green promise. But let us not be weary in well doing, for in due season we shall reap if we faint not.

DAVID LLOYD GEORGE.

THE MAN BEHIND THE GUNS

WHEN David Lloyd George, then an eager, alert, young candidate for the law, went to London to present himself for his final examination, he heard his first debate in Parliament. Gladstone had made a stirring, impassioned speech that completely cowed the Opposition leaders into silence; it seemed as if nothing more could be said. Then a slender young member arose, strode into the middle of the floor, snapped his fingers in the face of the Grand Old Man, and scornfully, vigorously, assailed his position. "I hated him for it," said Mr. Lloyd George years afterward, "I hated him, but I felt it was fine; it was splendid."

There spoke the man who dearly loved a fight for its own sake as well as for its cause. The greater the difficulty, the more powerful the adversary, the better he liked it. It was to him the real measure of a man and of the integrity of his convictions.

"Indifference is the great foe," he used to say.

"It is easier to let things alone than to bother about changing them. That is at bottom why all sorts of evils hold sway. Nobody cares enough to do anything. Then along comes a man with a strong conviction or two; he knows instinctively that the only way to get anything done is to raise a row. And being the sort that never runs away, he plunges in and wins."

Two years before the occasion of the Gladstone debate, on his first visit to the House of Commons, the lad of nineteen felt sure that he would one day have a place there. He wrote in his diary: "Went to the Houses of Parliament. Grand buildings outside, but inside very crabbed, small and suffocating, especially the House of Commons. I will not say but I eyed the assembly in a spirit similar to that in which William the Conqueror eyed England on his visit to Edward the Confessor as the region of his future domain. O vanity!"

It was more than ambition, however, stirring within the young Welshman that made him sure of his calling. There was also a very strong and definite resolution. For the two great passions of his soul—love of humanity and hatred of every form of tyranny and oppression—were strong within him even as a child, and when he arrived

124

at man's estate his work was waiting for him.

David Lloyd George was born January 17, 1863, in Manchester, England, where his Welsh father had gone to try his success at teaching. But not finding the opportunity for happy work and study of which he had dreamed, he turned back to the soil, hoping to regain his health and have more time for his books than there had been in the smoky city. He had hardly made his new start, however, when a sudden illness carried him away from his little family. . . . David's earliest memory was of a crowd gathered about his home. All their household goods—tables, chairs and beds—were piled out of doors with the plows, harrows, and other things that his father had used on the farm. How strange and pitiful they looked there in a heap on the grass! There was a noisy man standing by pointing at them, and then people began to carry them off. The light in the child's dark blue eyes changed from fear to anger as he saw some one pick up his favorite chair. With his sister's help he began to put stones under the gate to keep the people from getting out with all the things of their little world.

He was only three years old and he could not understand what it all meant, but he knew that his mother was very unhappy. He was sad, too, and lonely without his father. Then in the midst of their trouble came his uncle, Richard Lloyd, and somehow the world seemed a safe, warm place again.

"You are all coming to make a home with me—for me," he said to his sister.

It was a happy home in the little village of North Wales between the mountains and the sea. The cottage, made of stones taken from the fields, seemed truly a part of that beautiful land of craggy peaks, green meadows, and sparkling streams. It is small wonder that this seemed to David God's own country, and its sturdy people the very elect of the earth. For the boy's passionate love of mountains and glens was never a thing apart from his love of people. Like the Scotch poet he held that "an honest man's the noblest work of God"; and down deep in his heart he believed that Welsh people were a bit truer as well as a bit cleverer than other people.

Next to the cottage was the little shop with the sign "Richard Lloyd, Shoemaker" swinging over the door. His uncle was truly a wonderful man; he seemed to tower over all the other people as Snowdon rose over the other mountains. While he hammered away at his bench—for it took steady work to provide for three hungry children—he yet found time to take an interest in the joys and sorrows of his neighbors. . . . A farmer lad who was in disgrace for trapping a hare came in for counsel and comfort. It seemed that all the wild creatures of wood and field belonged exclusively to the squire, who cared more for his rights to the game than for the people who lived on his land. Another came to tell of his hard work to improve the soil and repair his house, and then how he had been told to leave the farm because he had refused to vote as the squire wished. It seemed that there were some people of privilege —people who could not even speak Welsh—who yet had the power to order all the ways of Welshmen, to tell them what to do, where to go to church and how to vote.

David was very proud of his uncle because he did not go to the church where the clergyman read prayers in English, but instead went to his own chapel at Criccieth, a mile distant. No one knew more about the Bible than his Uncle Richard, and no one knew more about the ways of the Government. Every evening David walked to Criccieth to get a copy of the Liverpool paper, and as he marched home, breathing in the air that had the tang of the ocean as well as the freshness of the mountains, he read with eager excitement the news of the war between Russia and Turkey; but when he got home and his uncle read the accounts of the debates in Parliament, that seemed even more interesting. He followed the fortunes of the big bills as if they were battles where the leaders of the parties were the generals. He gathered that the landowners were mostly Conservatives, that they wished to conserve the customs of the past with all their privileges of the present; and he knew that the Liberals were those who thought some changes were necessary in order to give the poor people a chance.

In 1868, there was an exciting election in that little corner of Wales; for the first time a Liberal carried the day. Then as an aftermath came notices to a number of the independent voters to quit their farms, for, so the papers read, "it is not right you should allow yourself to be led by others to vote against the interests of the estate on which you live and against the wishes of his lordship."

The memory of that glorious triumph when he had carried a flag and shouted himself hoarse was not more vivid in the child's mind than the tragedy which succeeded it of men turned out on the road-side because they had dared to vote as they thought right. That was, as he often said, his first memory of politics.

"The village smithy was my first parliament," he said. "Here we gathered on winter evenings in the red glow of the fire to discuss all the problems of Wales and her neighbors in this world and the next."

One can easily picture the scene,—the elderly smith, like a Druid majestic in his strength, and sitting about in the firelight the group of villagers discussing the daily news, religion and politics, and, when their spirits were high, taking up the refrain of one of the stirring Welsh airs. Is it any wonder that David, a boy who early gave proof of a keen mind and a quick wit, should have been much influenced by the talk of these stalwart men whose convictions came at white heat from the forge of hard experience?

Sometimes the magic of the firelight cast its spell on the imagination as the legends of Wales were told and the odes of the bards recited. There was the story of the Crags of the Eagles in whose shadow they lived. . . . Vortigern, an ancient

129

King of Britain, it was said, tried to build a stronghold on that spot but the stones refused to cleave together. Then the wizard, Merlin, bade him dig deep below the spot of his wall to find the reason of his defeat. There they discovered two sleeping dragons, one white and the other red. The first, Merlin said, was the symbol of the invading Saxons, while the other stood for the race of Britain. So it is that to this day the red dragon is the emblem of Wales, signifying its individual strength that refuses to be swallowed up or absorbed by any other nation. . . . The legends declared, too, that many heroes would come from the land of the Eagles to the defense of the fair hills and the green valleys of Wales. David may have dreamed that he was of the eagle brood; at any rate he knew that some day he would fight valiantly for the rights of his country. So it was that David Lloyd George, champion of the Welsh National Party, and defender of the downtrodden poor against class privilege and oppression, came into his own.

Before David had completed the course that the village school offered, Richard Lloyd had faced the question of his future. He knew that he had an exceptionally able lad in his keeping. "The

boy must have a chance," he said to his sister.
"He should by rights be a lawyer. I have a bit
of money laid by against the time I am too old
to work at my bench; that will serve to start our
David on his way."

But it was a long road to qualifying as a solicitor, and there were many fees; the money would
not stretch over all the demands. Richard Lloyd
saw the need of still further effort. Valiantly
he set himself to work with grammars and exer-
cise books to master the rudiments of Latin and
French in order that he might himself serve as
instructor to his nephew. Bravely they struggled
on together, and, when David was twenty-one
and the uncle's little pile of savings all spent, the
end for which they had labored was at hand. He
passed with honors his examinations and was en-
rolled as solicitor. There was only one lack—
three guineas to buy his lawyer's robe without
which he could not appear in the local courts.
"That is nothing," said David. "A few weeks'
humble work in an office shall furnish my garment
of dignity."

Young Lloyd George was an immediate success
as a solicitor. He really cared about his cases
and his clients, and he threw himself into his work

with energy and ardor. His keen mind at once seized the essential features and his ready wit enabled him to make the most of each point. At twenty-five he awoke to find himself famous for his daring and successful handling of a case that had attracted wide attention. He had proved himself a true champion of the poor against unreasonable customs and petty tyrannies.

Two years later, Lloyd George was sent to represent his home district in Parliament, defeating the squire of the countryside to whom as a boy he had deferentially touched his cap. Many said at the time, "The young upstart has had his little day. He thinks that his local success proves him a leader, but as he has gone up like a rocket he must come down like a stick." But the boy who at nineteen had looked down from the gallery at the House of Commons as the field of his future domain, knew that his career had only begun.

Lloyd George's early years in Parliament were in the main stormy ones. It seemed to many that he was desperately seeking notoriety by his rebel attitude even towards the leaders of his own party. A Liberal himself, he again and again dared to put himself and his championship of Wales to the fore against the leadership of the mighty Gladstone. And later when Joseph Chamberlain was the party chief, he moved that man of steel to wrath on more than one occasion.

It is only in the light of Lloyd George's whole career that we can judge aright those insurgent years when he seemed moved by "the imp of the perverse" to give as much trouble as possible. He was a man with a mission. Knowing as he did the wrongs of the poor, realizing how they were bound down by laws and customs which served the interests of those at the top, he was all afire with zeal to bring about some changes that would strike at the root of existing injustices. For instance the people of Wales should not be compelled to support an expensive established church, which they, as members of various other religious bodies, did not want. There should be home rule for Wales in order that all of her affairs might be directed by those immediately concerned. There should be better educational opportunities for the mass of the people. There should be readjustment of the burden of taxation which rested most heavily on those least able to bear it. These were some of the things for which he fought in season and out, for he could not abide leisurely, routine procedure when he was so fiercely alive to the needs of the people he had known all his life. And while he was looked upon by the leaders, who were working to carry out what they considered a safe and sane program for the welfare of the nation, as a most presumptuous and uncomfortable member, his influence began to be felt. It was generally conceded that he was a force to be reckoned with.

During those years of struggle Lloyd George was growing. While ever an ardent champion of Wales, he was able now to see beyond the horizon of local interests and embrace in his sympathies the problems that concerned the country at large. It was soon evident, moreover, that he was able to take a still broader view, and consider the affairs of his nation in relation to the rights of other peoples. His attitude at the time of the Boer War showed this larger understanding and at the same time proved that his sympathy with the under dog was stronger than any self interest.

For a time Lloyd George was the best hated man in England. He dared to declare that his country was wrong in making war against a small, struggling people even though there had been much cause for provocation. He showed that his patriotism was not of the kind that says "My

country always, right or wrong!'' But feeling
was running high in England just then, and in
the heat of the moment he could only seem a
traitor to the land that had nurtured him. When
he dared to appear in the home town of Chamberlain to attack his war policy the fury of the
people passed all bounds. A riot ensued and the
rash Welshman narrowly escaped a violent end
by getting out of the hall in the clothes of a policeman, who found that only in this way was the
protection of the law of any avail. The general
feeling may be indicated by a remark made to
Mr. Chamberlain.

"So your friends were not able to get rid of
Lloyd George the other night," said a member
of the House in passing his chief in the lobby.

"What is everybody's business is nobody's
business," replied Mr. Chamberlain with a real
glint in his eyes.

The sure place that this unpopular statesman
held with his own people was proved by the fact
that he was reelected in the very midst of the
general hue and cry. The public gasped. They
wouldn't have expected that even of an obscure
little corner like Wales. And it was not long
before another surprise was upon them. The

new Liberal Premier, Sir Henry Campbell-Bannerman, picked out Lloyd George for one of the minor positions in his cabinet—president of the Board of Trade. What could a sane man be thinking about to put an untamed free-lance and hotblood like Lloyd George in any post of responsibility?

"We must have new blood—men who will not be afraid to blaze new trails," said the Prime Minister.

It was soon evident that they had such a man in the little Welshman. He proved unexpectedly that he was something more than an agitator—a man who could think things out clearly to a finish and then work ahead until something was actually done. It seemed that he was capable of solid, constructive work; and that, moreover, he could deal with people in a new way. Belligerency had given place to tact and courtesy. His skill in handling a labor crisis which threatened to tie up all the railroads in the United Kingdom won for him general acclaim. Facing the question fairly from the standpoint of the needs of the country as well as that of the rights of the workers, he threw himself into the breach with a fervor and

DAVID LLOYD GEORGE
Premier of Great Britain

persuasive reasonableness that won concessions from both sides.

The old daring originality was, however, by no means lost in the sober effectiveness of the new minister's work. It was said that under his control the office was proving not only the most active but also the most interesting position in the cabinet. But even so, the public was hardly prepared for the next step. When Campbell-Bannerman died in 1908, his successor, Mr. Asquith, promoted Lloyd George to the position of Chancellor of the Exchequer, the post of second importance in the cabinet.

It was a sudden, dazzling honor, but I do not think it was that which brought the gleam to the dark blue eyes of the shoemaker's boy. At last he was to have an opportunity to really better the condition of the people from whom he sprang, whose needs he felt as did no other leader.

This is the way he went about his reforms: As Chancellor he was called upon to prepare a Budget of the public money to be expended, and a schedule of taxation to meet this outlay. Lloyd George's Budget of 1909 was an affair of such far-reaching importance that it not only introduced some radical measures like old age pensions and workmen's insurance against illness and unemployment, but it shifted a large part of the burden of taxes on to the rich by greatly increasing the rate on large incomes, inheritances, land profits, and coal mines. In concluding his explanation of his scheme, Mr. Lloyd George said: "This, Mr. Chairman, is a war Budget. It is for raising money to wage war against poverty. I cannot help hoping and believing that before this generation has passed away we shall have advanced a great step toward that good time when poverty and wretchedness, and the human degradation which always follows in their camp, will be as remote from the people of this country as the wolves which once infested its forests."

The next day all England was talking of the amazing Chancellor. The laboring classes hailed him as a Daniel; the well-to-do classes called him a pick-pocket. Thinking the country was with them, the House of Lords decided to put on a bold front and kill the Budget, but by so doing they signed their own death warrant. The cabinet was dissolved and another election called. Then the Lords found themselves not only obliged to pass the hated Budget, but also compelled to assent to a bill forfeiting a large part of their ancient privileges. Never again could they hold up a bill passed by the elected representatives of the people; and, moreover, *any* bill passed by three sessions of the Commons might become a law over their heads. The will of the people was to rule. And the man who had made England "safe for democracy" was Lloyd George.

Then came the World War. When Belgium was invaded England entered the field on the side of outraged humanity. Freedom should not perish from the earth. But at first all did not face the situation fairly; to some it seemed that England might well hold aloof, keeping in her own pleasant ways of peace and prosperity. Some of the cabinet ministers resigned, and everybody waited for Lloyd George to follow their lead. They remembered his speeches at the time of the Boer War; he was a peace-at-any-price man, they said. Many exulted, "Now we shall be rid forever of the firebrand." One peer promised the people on his estate that he would celebrate with them the day Lloyd George stepped down by a barbecue. Other people shook their heads; "If he goes the country will lose a tremendous power," they said. But Lloyd George did not resign. Still everybody waited in suspense for a word from him; and when it was announced that he was to speak it seemed as if the whole city tried to get within hearing. That night the peace-loving Welshman gave the most rousing call-to-arms that England had heard.

"There is no man," he said, "who has always regarded the prospect of engaging in a great war with greater reluctance than I have done through all my political life. There is no man more convinced that we could not have avoided it now without dishonor." He went on with all his might pouring out the vials of his wrath upon the war-makers who were marching over the rights of a helpless little nation. He spoke of the riotous meeting when the war party at home had threatened him violence. "At that meeting," he said, "I tried to stand against the idea that great and powerful empires ought to have the right to crush small nationalities. I might have been right, or I might have been wrong, but the principle which drove me to resist even our own country is the one that has brought me here to support my country."

But it was not only by his speeches that Lloyd George was fighting. As Chancellor of the Exchequer he sent out an appeal to the leading financiers of the country: "This country is thrown into financial chaos," he said. "I want the assistance of the best brains of expert people. I want you to give me your help as to the best way of putting things straight."

Then a dramatic thing happened. The men who had most berated the wicked Budget went to confer quietly with its creator. They found themselves talking freely with one who was frankly eager to be instructed. Then, seizing the essential points with his usual clear-headedness, the Finance Minister went out and told the people about the confusion that war had brought to the banks and business houses, and the need of special measures to tide them over. It was all explained so clearly that a child could comprehend. Now all the men of finance were calling down blessings on the head of Lloyd George. It was seen that the bold and original methods that he devised had gone to the core of the difficulty and warded off a business crisis that would have served the enemy as well as a defeat in the field.

Everybody knows how disheartening the first year of the war was. Why could not the Allies with their combined might effect more and bring the struggle to a swift conclusion? Lloyd George

141

was one of those who faced the problem squarely:
He saw that while there was no lack of brave soldiers there was pitiful lack of proper munitions.
The men had no way of replying in kind to the
high explosive shells of the enemy. He saw that
the old over-cautious, muddling policy that he had
rebelled against in time of peace when he longed
to put through some measure for the people's good
was the thing which now in time of war was crip-
pling the army in the field. Once again he dared
to attack openly those in control, even when it
meant a serious criticism of the people's hero,
Lord Kitchener. But there must be more guns
and more shells. The men must not be sacrificed
and the war must be won.

The Government then said in effect to Lloyd
George, "We will see what you can do." He was
moved from the position of Chancellor of the Exchequer to a new post created for him. As Minister of Munitions he was given power to put the
industries of the country on a war basis that
would make them equal to the demands of the
moment.

"Shells, more shells, mightier shells, and still
more shells!" was the cry. The country was
thoroughly aroused. It was at once plain that

142

the munition plants were hopelessly inadequate. Lloyd George saw that he must enlist the services of all the people and the equipment of all the factories and engineering firms. New men must be trained; women must be prepared to take up the work. Manufacturers and business men were called to consult with the new minister to devise how every plant which could produce shells or parts of shells might serve the country's need. Soon factories that had been making plows, sewing-machines, automobiles and many other things were turning out shells—only shells. So the tools of peace had become the sinews of war.

There were other problems, however, besides taking a census of all the machines in the country and enlisting the cooperation of all the manufacturers. Each plant must work at top steam and each worker must prove efficient. That meant that the drink problem must be dealt with and the health of the workers safeguarded. It also meant that the rules governing labor must be set aside.

"Our Munition Minister will meet his Waterloo there," people said. "The trades unions will never yield an inch."

Lloyd George called special meetings of the men. "An enlisted workman," he said, "cannot choose his battle-field or the time he is to fight. If a house is on fire you can't say that you are not liable to serve at three o'clock in the morning. You can't choose the hour. You can't argue as to whose duty it is to carry the water-bucket and whose duty it is to put it into a crackling furnace. You must put the fire out.'' The workers understood and responded heartily to a man.

It seemed as if the country had now fallen into the habit of turning to Lloyd George in time of stress. When a strike broke out in the Welsh mines which supplied the Navy with coal, and the Board of Trade despaired of effecting a compromise, Lloyd George was called upon. He went, talked with the employers and men face to face, and conquered. When, at the death of Lord Kitchener, the question arose, ''Where shall we find a Minister of War?'' the answer came, ''There is only one man—Lloyd George.''

Lloyd George was indeed the man of the hour. He frequently visited the trenches and went to Paris for direct consultation with the commanders. He sensed the needs of the time—regulation of food and fuel supplies and elimination of luxuries; also Government control of railways, shipping, and munition works. He realized the need of a greater army and forced on conscription. His greatest individual work, however, as Minister of War, was the organizing of the railway system behind the British army in France.

When in December, 1916, the country was aroused to the need of a strong hand at the helm, a man for war time who would act quickly and vigorously, the King asked Lloyd George to serve as Prime Minister.

"If you take a job do it with all your might," cried Lloyd George. "We must see the war through, and there must be no hugger-mugger peace. It must be an end where we can see light after the dark struggle."

One of his first acts was to create a special War Council, men without administrative responsibility who were given supreme control in managing the country's business. New departments in charge of shipping, and labor were filled not from the ranks of political leaders but from the men who had made good in business or public administration during the stress of war. He called into being the Imperial War Cabinet representing England's colonies; and, more important than all, he not only realized keenly the need of unity of command for the Allied Armies, but he also had the courage to see the matter through. The creation, first of a Supreme War Council of the Allies, and later the selection of General Foch as Commander-in-Chief, came as the direct result of his insistence.

There was a terrible hue and cry at the time of his famous "brutally frank" speech in Paris. "He has attacked his own country in time of war," it was said. "He has given aid and encouragement to the enemy."—"Now the power of this upstart will be pricked like a big bubble," said his opponents.

But after the dust of the fray had somewhat cleared, Lloyd George was seen standing erect and confident, still the man of the hour.

"I made up my mind to take risks," he said, "and I took them, to arouse public sentiment, not here merely, but in France, in Italy, and in America. It is not easy to rouse public opinion. I may know nothing of military strategy, but I do know something of political strategy. To raise a row is the only way to get a job through. I determined to make a disagreeable speech that would force everybody to talk about this scheme, and they have talked about it. The result is that America is in, Italy is in, France is in, Britain is in, and public opinion is in, and that is vital."

THE MAN BEHIND THE GUNS

So Lloyd George stuck by his guns, and "fired the shot heara round the world." But the man who was, perhaps, the greatest power behind the guns that won the war, is truly a man of peace. He looks ahead to the sane work of reconstruction that will make the world a better place for all peoples.

"We believe with Lincoln," he said, "that our armies are ministers of good, not evil. Through all the carnage and suffering and conflicting motives of the Civil War, Lincoln held steadfastly to the belief that it was the freedom of the people to govern themselves which was the fundamental issue at stake. So do we to-day. For when the people of central Europe accept the peace which is offered them by the Allies, not only will the allied peoples be free, as they have never been free before, but the German people, too, will find that in losing their dream of an empire over others, they have found self-government for themselves."

CRUSADERS OF THE WAR:

I

THE LIBERATOR OF BAGDAD

Think, in this batter'd Caravanserai
Whose Portals are alternate Night and Day,
  How Sultan after Sultan with his pomp
Abode his destin'd Hour and went his way.

They say the Lion and the Lizard keep
The Courts where Jamshyd gloried and drank deep:
  And Bahram, that great Hunter—the Wild Ass
Stamps o'er his Head, but cannot break his Sleep.
                              OMAR KHAYYAM.

I

GENERAL MAUDE

MESOPOTAMIA—the Land between the Rivers, the garden-spot of Eden where human life first came to its own, where great empires rose and passed away before the glories of Greece and Rome were even thought of—Mesopotamia, with your ancient splendor and present desolation, why did the nations choose you as the scene of one act of the terrible war tragedy?

"If they had to fight somewhere, I suppose it was good they hit upon this place where there is nothing they can upset in the fray," said a Y. M. C. A. worker. "When we growl about the beastly climate, let's stop to think about what is happening to France and then ask ourselves whether we'd like to call down that blight on any other fair spot of the earth."

"Yes, you bet we can put up with the 115 plus in the shade, the mosquitoes, sand-fleas, and all the other ten plagues, if it really helps to put an end to that awfulness,'' responded a companion who believed that peace is a blessing worth fighting for.

Yet how did it really come about? Nobody saw much that was promising in Mesopotamia. (Mespot the soldiers called it.) Wandering Arabs pitched a tent here to-day to be off to-morrow. The Turks had no use for it; once they offered it to England as a gift if that nation would relieve them of the control. But at the time Britain saw nothing in the offer—why assume a bootless responsibility?

No one could imagine any good coming out of that desert land of summer heat and winter sand blasts. Therefore the world was somewhat mystified to hear that William II of Germany was planning to build a railroad across the country of desolation to Bagdad, and England realized that the project could mean nothing but a threat to her influence in India and the East. Why, for profitable commerce, should the route avoid districts of agricultural promise in order to take the shortest cut across the desert? The military advantage of such a highway was only toc apparent. It was perfectly transparent to the Arab Sheikh of Kuweit, who in his friendship for Great Britain, obstinately refused, notwithstanding all the pressure that Turkey could bring to bear, to grant or sell the privilege to run such a road through his territory.

The friendship between Turkey and the German emperor dates some years back of the war alliance. In 1889, the Kaiser took occasion to visit Constantinople and establish friendly relations with the Sultan and his people, paving the way for the peaceful invasion of the Ottoman Empire by German agents and traders. In 1898, he made a tour through Palestine as the special friend and ally of the Turk, even on one remarkable occasion in Damascus, proclaiming himself "Defender of Islam." Many pictures of the Prussian monarch in Turkish garments were left behind as souvenirs, and in referring to them some of the German diplomatic agents whispered confidentially that his majesty was at heart a sincere convert to Islamism. On the summit of the Mount of Olives he built a huge, hideously pretentious structure with a statue of himself in coat-of-mail as a crusader dominating the court-yard. This monument to an autocrat's vanity was built to serve two ends. First, it provided a hospice for German pilgrims to Jerusalem; so much for the present and the public. Second, it harbored cunningly devised machine gun emplacements which would command the approaches to the hill; so much for the possible future and those who shared the Kaiser's dream of world empire.

"It is indeed an ill wind which blows no one any good," said an English officer, "and the Kaiser's attempt to win control in the East which brought the war to the Garden of Eden may lead to the restoration of that lost paradise."

"What can possibly be done for a land that is either desert or swamp, with the extremes of parching heat and unruly floods?" he was challenged.

"In ancient times there was a system of irrigation that met both difficulties," he replied, "and the man who has made a study of the present condition assures us that it can be done again by an employment of some engineering skill and sufficient capital. The blight that has come upon that naturally fertile land is the result of the shiftless, plundering methods of Turkish control —nothing done for the up-keep or improvement of the countries they are supposed to govern."

Even while the destruction of war was going forward some of the life-giving, up-building forces were at work, which made the Englishman prophesy that the desert would one day blossom as the rose and the wastes become fields of waving grain. "Life is ever Lord of Death" and the law of growth more powerful than man's blind, puny efforts to destroy. In the very carrying forward of the war it was necessary to extend railways; build bridges, stations, and freight-depots; and improve the navigation of the Tigris. The needs of the army led both to the employment of the people and the extension of irrigation. This meant a change for the better in the condition of the lawless, wandering Arabs, and the beginning of a government that insured order, the protection of just laws, and the possibility of free development. The modern well-equipped port of Basra, with its hard-surfaced roads, warehouses, piers and dry-docks, may be taken as a type and promise of the new order.

But the beginning of the story has to do with the old Basra, where four British transports from Bombay landed a little force of Tommies and Indian troops in November, 1914. They found a wretchedly unsanitary Turkish-Arab town—no docks, warehouses, roads, vehicles, lights, or civilized comforts of any sort. They saw in every direction a stretch of drab and tawny desert through which wriggled in a particularly unpleasant, tortuous way two shallow, sluggish, brown rivers, along whose banks grew files of tall, fringing date palms—the only green that broke the desolate expanse.

"What are we to do in this bloomin' spot?" asked one indignant Tommy. "This is n't the war I'm after!"

"Well," drawled a comrade, "you remember some chap once said that war was hell; this looks like it, does n't it?"

"What are we supposed to do here anyway?" persisted Tommy.

" 'Ours not to question why,' " quoted the other. "But since we 're at war with the Turks, I suppose we 're bound to get at them where we can. You know what the order said, that we 're sent 'to safeguard our interests and to protect the friendly Arabs.' I don't know what the 'interests' are besides the oil-works over yonder and the pipe-lines up to the oil fields. There would be something doing though if they took a notion to drop a bomb there."

"Well," pursued Master Tommy, "of course even I can see that the Navy must have a place to

tap oil in this part of the world,—but say, did you
ever see a 'friendly Arab'?''

The early experiences of the soldiers tended to
impress them with the trickery and treachery of
their new neighbors. Many were the tales told
of their thievishness. One man had had his kit
taken; another had been relieved of everything,
even his tent, while he slept. An Indian sentry,
challenging in vain a skulking shade from the
desert, fired and brought down his man; but as he
stooped to look at him the tables were turned.
The Arab sprang to his feet, snatched the sentry's
gun and made off with it through the night.

There were, however, some good Arabs, the soldiers were assured. There were many who had
been loyal to the English at a time when the Turks,
urged on by the Germans, had tried to work on
their religious zeal to bring about a "holy war."
The whole world waited breathless because the
jihah was held to be a duty of true Moslems. But
the Arabs remembered that it was to the English
and not the Turks that they had looked for protection from pirates when they went to sell the
fruits of their pearling season. The Britons were
the strong men of earth, and strength was to man
as swiftness to a horse. The sheikhs had a fine

157

scorn of the indolent Turks who made such a poor
pretense of governing. Many of the Arabs, moreover, belonged to a sect of the Mohammedans who
held that the Sultan was not the true heir to the
authority of their Prophet, but that the rightful
descendants had been slain.

"But we must play a safe game in Mesopotamia," the soldiers were warned. "With the
Arabs as with the people of Egypt and India, the
battle is to the strong. It is only as leaders that
they hold to us; at the first sign of weakening they
drop away."

Basra was not taken without a struggle—the
first real grapple with the enemy and the enemy's
country. Of the two the latter seemed far more
formidable, though the Turks were unpleasant
enough. But picture indefinite stretches of hope-
less swamp, fringed with date palms and grape-
vine entanglements, through which ran canals and
creeks, where Turks fought from ambush behind
the trees and under the banks of the ditches.
Fancy marching twenty-eight miles through
slimy mud in one day. That was the "wicked,
bad campaigning" that tried the souls of the
Tommies. But there they were in Basra, with
the Turks in retreat up the river toward Bag-

dad and away from the precious Anglo-Persian oil properties at Abadan—the little island at the mouth of the Shatt-el-Arab, as the estuary which carries the combined waters of the Tigris and Euphrates into the Persian Gulf is called.

Then came the first ill-fated expedition to Bagdad. Beginning with successes that led the British to underestimate both the strength of the enemy and their own serious handicap in the matter of communications and supplies, they were lured on from Amara, one hundred and thirty-two miles up the Tigris from Basra, and then a hundred and fifty miles further to Kut-el-Amara, which commanded the direct routes into Persia. It seemed impossible to hold back with another victory beckoning at the next bend in the river, especially as a halt might be read as weakness.

It was the British way to dare splendidly, and there is no wine so heady as that of unmixed success. The important position of Kut was taken and occupied by a gallant charge that fairly swept the Turks out in confusion towards Bagdad. What more natural than the next move? "We pursued the routed Turks with the utmost vigor" reads the official report, and it may be added, with such momentum that they never paused until they were half-way between Kut and Bagdad. Was it strange that the cry "On to Bagdad!" should have put to silence the voice of prudence: "Remember that you are running ahead of your supply bases; the safe game is the only one to play in this unknown, untamed country. Don't forget that 'an army travels on its stomach'; if it tries to get up and run, it may not live to run another day!"

We are told that General Townshend listened to the promptings of caution. He was a seasoned officer who had fought on the Nile and in South Africa. Now he sent airplanes ahead to learn the strength of the enemy, and reported: "On military grounds we should consolidate our position at Kut." But the cry "On to Bagdad!" swept all before it. Why let the routed Turks retire and recover? The men were eager to be up and after them, and the orders came to follow up the victory. Bagdad was a prize worth the winning. It would bring thousands of Arabs to the support of the conquerors of the sacred city; it would mean such a blow to Turkey that she would hardly be able to rally her forces against Suez or India.

In the shadow of the ruined Arch of Ctesiphon— symbol of the vanished glories of the past—there was a mighty struggle with the entrenched Turks, and again the British won. They were almost within reach of the goal when the tide turned. The Turks were reenforced from Bagdad in such numbers that they threatened to surround General Townshend's little army. There was nothing to do but to retire to Kut and wait for men and munitions.

Then followed the siege. For one hundred and forty-three days General Townshend held out against the enemy before he surrendered—not to force of arms but to famine. Day after day he heard the guns of the rescuing party who were struggling in vain to reach Kut, held back in their advance against the Turks by the fearful mire of the rainy season. Then a part of the heroic little band knew the bitterness of going up the river past the scenes of their former triumphs to the city of the Arabian Nights as prisoners. The drum-beat "On to Bagdad" was muffled now.

The man whose task it was to turn defeat into victory, General Sir Stanley Maude, was put in command August 28, 1916. "The smallest part of a general's work is done at the time of battle," he said. "That victory belongs to the men who go over the top. The test of the commander comes

161

in laying the foundation of the campaign, in the planning for success and the providing against failure.''

General Maude spent four months in his preparations, and the results of his work were to be seen in many places besides in the camps of the soldiers, who had to be made fit for vigorous campaigning after the ills and torments of the most savage summer and the depressing effects of defeat. But their "Army Commander" led them out of the Egyptian darkness of weakness and indifference into the Promised Land of spirited action. Like Kipling's efficient sergeant who could "drill a black man white," he got his Tommies in trim by putting them to work. Only a small detachment were left on the fighting line opposite the Turk's confident position at Sunnaiyat below Kut where the rescuing party had been held while General Townshend fought starvation. The rest of the troops were told off to assist in the great work of preparedness,—building roads, docks and warehouses, and helping in the moving of supplies. One felt the strength of General Maude's influence with his men and their whole-hearted confidence in him when they spoke his name or stood at salute before his six-feet-three of commanding presence. "Every inch a general!" they used to say proudly, "Nothing gets by *him*."

But the most conspicuous result of the Army Commander's generalship was seen in the way the dogged British habit of "getting things done" had struck root in Mesopotamia. Witness the new Basra, with its docks, warehouses and hospitals; witness the roads that conquered the mud of the rainy months. Along the river bank where the stores were landed was a hard-surfaced oiled way which the men pointed out with pardonable pride. "You 'd better appreciate the going along here; it 's the most expensive six-miles in the world," they would say. "Every bit of the paving material brought from the interior of India!" Later some road-making material nearer at hand was unearthed, but that six-mile stretch will remain a perfect type of the way the British were overriding obstacles under the leadership of "the Man of Mesopotamia."

Eleanor Franklin Egan, in her delightfully vivid account of many phases of the Bagdad campaign, "The War in the Cradle of the World," has a really epic chapter on the calling of the river boats from the various streams of the British dominions to do special duty on the Tigris in the nation's

163

hour of need. Only the humble craft made for shallow channels might serve here in the important work of carrying supplies and removing the wounded. So the "penny steamers" of the Thames, and their colonial cousins from the Nile, the Ganges, and South Africa, steamed away from their familiar haunts and crossed the seas to answer the call. I cannot refrain from quoting a few lines from that Odyssey of the Penny Steamers:

River boats were an absolute, a primary necessity. They could not be built in Mesopotamia, nor anywhere else in time to relieve the desperate situation. . . .

Then they would have to come out of other rivers otherwheres and make their various ways somehow—no matter how!—across the seas and up through the Persian Gulf! . . . It has been one of the bravest and strangest achievements of the war, and one hears with a feeling of specially chill regret that more than eighty of them have failed! A few from everywhere have gone—along with the high hopes of British sailors, and usually with the sailors, too—to the bottom of the seas they were never meant to venture on. . . . As I watched the curious, flat-bottomed, high-funneled, doubledecked, paddle-wheeled little craft churning briskly downstream I was seeing visions of the kind of heroism that makes one prayerful. . . .

General Maude's "safe game" included the building of a railroad that was to be the measure of their advance. "Only what an army can grapple with steel rails is safely theirs," he said. So they never went beyond rail-head.

There are many curious stories told of the way the desert mirage mixed things up in the Mesopotamian battles. One saw phantom armies, clouds of galloping men riding across the shimmering sand, who disappeared into air, as did the cooling lakes under sheltering palms that seemed to lie just beyond the thirsty traveler. "It was terribly upsetting to a chap's nerve as well as to his aim," said one of the men. "And of course you can see how it played hob with our calculation of gun ranges. But once it gave us a victory that was like a miracle out of the Bible. At the very moment that the Turks seemed to have us beyond hope of rescue, lo and behold! they turned and fled like mad! They thought they saw reenforcements coming over the desert—hosts upon hosts— and would you believe it?—it was just a little supply and ambulance train moving along in its own little cloud of dust that the desert light had played upon until it seemed 'terrible as an army with banners.' They say the unlucky Turkish commander committed suicide when he learned how they had been bewitched."

There was going to be no chance for any sort

of a mirage to lure General Maude away from a safe game. From the planning of supply trains and depots along the path of his advance to the installing of ice-plants and special hospital tents for the treatment of men suffering from heat-strokes, each factor of the Mesopotamian situation was weighed and dealt with in turn.

The Turks felt that they, too, were playing a safe game. Reenforced in men, and in morale— the fruit of victory,—they waited in strongly en-trenched positions at Sunnaiyat on the north bank of the Tigris and further west at the Hai, a stream flowing due south from Kut. It was their object to hold their own with a comparatively small force by virtue of their carefully guarded positions, and then get behind the British to strike at India through Persia. The Sunnaiyat was indeed well taken. A wedge-shaped strip of land between an impassable morass and the Tigris, it was insured against flank attacks, and protected by a remark-able system of trenches, bristling with gun-pits, mines, and barbed wire entanglements.

It was General Maude's plan to begin by a bom-bardment at Sunnaiyat designed merely to give the Turks something to think about while he struck boldly on the other side of the river, crossing the

Hai by a surprise attack. Then, through a series of hammering blows he hoped to seize the enemy's system of trenches there, and, crossing the Tigris at the weakest part of the line, as far west as possible, threaten the communication of the enemy at Sunnaiyat. Thus the Turks might be compelled to yield that stronghold in order to preserve the life-line of supplies from Bagdad.

The plan worked well. By the middle of December, General Maude had the main body of his forces concentrated on the south side of the river with all detachments trained on the enemy positions there, and on the night of the thirteenth the mighty push against Kut was launched—just one year after the time that General Townshend and his men took their plucky stand in that city. In spite of all the enemy's well-laid plans, in spite of the most adverse weather conditions—a time of midday heat followed by marrow-piercing cold at night, and sand-storms which ushered in the season of flooding rains that reduced the fighting ground to quagmires—in spite of all the preventions of man and the perversities of nature, they passed on to success.

In the crossing of the Tigris above Kut the British seemed to achieve the impossible. After two

months of vigorous hammering that drove the
Turks back inch by inch from the country around
the Hai, they took refuge in the positions about
Kut on the opposite side of the river and in their
impregnable field of Sunnaiyat, as who should say,
"Thus far and no farther! Here we can hold till
doomsday!"

But the day of doom was already dawning.
This is the way the account of it read in General
Maude's official report:

The waterlogged state of the country and a high flood on
the Tigris now necessitated a pause, but the time was use-
fully employed in methodical preparation for the passage of
the Tigris at Shumran. Positions, guns and machine-gun
crews to support the crossing were selected, approaches and
ramps were made, and crews were trained to man the pontoons. In order to keep our intentions concealed it was necessary that most of the details, including the movement of
guns, should be carried out under the cover of night. Opposite Sunnaiyat where it was intended to renew the assault,
artillery barrages were carried out daily in order to induce
the enemy to expect such barrages unaccompanied by an assault as part of the daily routine. Minor diversions were also
planned to deceive the enemy as to the point at which it was
intended to cross the river.

"We have waited for the rain and mud to stop
you," said one of the 2,000 prisoners who had not
succeeded in making good their crossing of the

SIR FREDERICK STANLEY MAUDE
The late Lieutenant-General and Commander-in-Chief in Mesopotamia

river to Kut, "but Kismet willed that it should not rain." And when Fate sent the longed-for torrent just a bit too late, it had clogged their feet as they tried to flee. Clearly Kismet was with the British, for not only before the flood but through the mire they pressed on.

Only madmen would have attempted to cross the river, so the Turks thought—the river at flood which was three hundred and fifty yards wide at the point where the ferries and pontoons were thrown over, swept by the machine-gun fire from the commanding positions of the enemy. Cannon to right of them; cannon to left of them! "But we did it!" exulted one Tommy from his hospital cot; he had no hand to bring to salute but his face glowed. . . . "The men pressed on with unconquerable valor and determination," wrote the Army Commander.

Well, what use of holding out against Kismet! Turks at least know enough not to strive against Fate. When on the evening of February 23, that fatal bridge built in nine hours across the Tigris at flood was ready for the triumphal passing of General Maude's men, the Turkish forces were in full retreat toward Bagdad, fighting defiantly every step of the way. "It's not your infidel strength that has won," they seemed to say. "Kismet has willed it."

The armies of the three elements—earth, air, and water—were warring together now against the routed Turks. Airplanes made swooping attacks dropping death from above; gun-boats advanced along the river shelling the defenses along the banks; and the invincible army pressed on. With just one pause half-way to Bagdad to insure lines of communication and the best organization of the troops, they advanced toward the goal— eighteen miles one day, seventeen miles the next. "On to Bagdad" was now a mighty trumpet call.

In the City of Golden Domes, of minarets, and magic associations of oriental romance—a city of splendid dreams; in the unsanitary, unsightly collection of mud-dwellings and gaudy bazaars— a city of sordid reality—for Bagdad was both of these—there was tremendous excitement. The Turks were fleeing; why did not the British come and keep order? For the terrible Kurds were seizing the moment of confusion for looting and outrages of every sort. "The British are at our gates; why do they not enter?" moaned the Arabian traders who saw their rugs and precious inlaid furniture scattered about and destroyed as the robbers seized and fought among themselves for the jewelry and costly bric-a-brac.

When the Tommies at last entered the city, pale and haggard from sleepless nights and hard fighting, they found the streets crowded with a host of people in holiday attire—men in turbans, red fezzes, and Persian-lamb caps and long, girdled robes; women in silk draperies, fancy slippers and festive lace veils. Arabs, Armenians, Persians, Syrians, Jews, joined in the great rejoicing. Their deliverers who would insure freedom and protection for all had come.

Many were disappointed that General Maude did not seize the opportunity for a triumphal entry. Surely there might have been some satisfying flourish after all the weary struggle! But that was not the Army Commander's way, nor was it in keeping with the British spirit. He left it for the results—and the people of Bagdad—to do the cheering. A few troops entered the city to patrol the streets and preserve order. For himself he had them moor his floating headquarters on one of the supply-boats to the wall of the British Residency, and accompanied by the members of his staff, walked quietly ashore "as casually as he might have done had he been only a very tired traveler arriving under the most ordinary circumstances," it was remarked.

They did not at once, however, take calm and assured possession. Bagdad must be made forever safe from the domination of the Turk; victory must be made sure. To insure the city against a rallying counter-attack, the famous Scottish Black Watch pursued the routed enemy through dust storms, and desperate fighting that lasted two nights and a day,—for the Turks were stubborn in their defiance. They must bow to Kismet, but they hated the instruments of his will. The resolute conduct of the rank and file in face of defeat won the admiration of the Tommies. "If there's fighting to be done, give me Johnny Turk," they said. "He will 'stick it' to the finish!"

But the end had indeed come on March 10, 1917, when General Maude entered Bagdad. The prestige of the Turks with the Arabs was gone, and with it all hope of striking a blow at the English in India. All the cultivated lands of Babylonia and the prospect of their harvests for provisioning the armies of the Central Powers had slipped away. Inspired by the Turkish defeat in Meso-

potamia, the Arabs of Hedjaz, a province of
Turkey in Asia, revolted and proclaimed their independence under the leadership of the Shereef of
Mecca who captured the Turkish garrisons in that
sacred city, secured the allegiance of the orthodox
Arabs and Syrians whose religious zeal had been
outraged by the Young Turks, and took the title of
King of Hedjaz. Several Turkish towns were
seized and the Syrian railway seriously crippled.

While Bagdad was still celebrating the coming
of the English and the dawn of its new day of
freedom a sudden hush fell upon the general rejoicing. The conquerors had a staggering loss.
After three days of illness General Maude died on
November 18, 1917, of the pestilence of the country—cholera—taken, it was said, from the raw
milk he had poured into his coffee at a Jewish reception in honor of the victory.

"The Huns have scored again," was the bitter
word that passed from one group of soldiers to
the next as they looked at each other with white,
set faces. "Who will 'carry on' now?"

Then, as they repeated in hushed voices the last
words of their beloved Army Commander, "Tell
them I can't come to the office to-day. They must
just carry on,"—they knew that they *would* "carry

on,'' with the undying spirit of their leader urging them forward. For the cause of freedom and peace does not depend on the strength of any one man, but on the might of unnumbered hosts ever carrying on.

General Marshall, the corps commander of the eastern front, succeeded General Maude. ''He will see that the Army Commander's plans are carried through,'' said one of the officers. ''You know he used to insist that Marshall was the better general of the two. 'He's a wonderful leader,' he once said; 'wish I could work things out with the sweep he does. Being an office man clips your power. Marshall has had the service in the field and the touch with the men that are the real thing.' ''

General Maude's successor did indeed carry on. By swift, skilful blows he swept the Turks from the region of the Euphrates, destroying all their hopes of rallying there for the recapture of Bagdad, drove them a hundred miles further along the Tigris, cleared them out of their boasted strategic position on the Persian frontier, and strengthened the barrier along that front which had threatened to collapse on the retirement of Russia from the war.

THE LIBERATOR OF BAGDAD

When one reviews the Mesopotamian story from its dashing promise that ended in the tragedy at Kut, through the second campaign where the steady, four-square generalship of Maude triumphed in a series of engagements that must set a standard for all future colonial commanders, to the final capitulation of the Turks when General Townshend was released to carry to the Allies the white flag of surrender, one is struck by the undaunted British will to "carry on" that alone made it possible. And one kindles at the thought that "Peace hath her victories no less renowned than war"; and that in the reclaiming of the desert, in the development of the country through the freedom and enlightenment of its peoples, the spirit that commands victory will still "carry on."

CRUSADERS OF THE WORLD WAR:

II

THE DELIVERER OF JERUSALEM

"Palestine has been of greater significance to mankind, spiritually and materially, than any other single country in the world. . . . Nowhere else has so much history run into or through so narrow a space."

II

GENERAL ALLENBY

"WHEN the river Nile flows into Palestine, there will come a prophet from the west who shall drive the Turk from Jerusalem," so ran the Arab prophecy; and one of the most interesting chapters in the story of the World War is concerned with its fulfilment.

The greatest events of human history, like the most momentous happenings in the life of every individual, come to pass so quietly, so inevitably, that we do not perceive their trend any more than we see the growth of a tree. We know the sapling; we sit in the shade of the tree and eat of its fruit. The results are ours, but not the alchemy that has changed earth and air into food for man.

Was there any one during the first dark months of war who could see how the nations were being led? In particular, had the great captains of England any vision of the part their armies should have in the freeing of Jerusalem, the holy city of

179

three religions? Let us see what it was that gave rise to the last and greatest of the crusades.

In the early days of the great struggle the whole thought of England, as of her allies, was centered upon the Western front. How could there be any question that the country that the invader had seized was the place where the war must be fought out and the victory won? There were, however, those who before long began to say that Britain was singularly blind to the situation at her eastern gate. It is here, they sounded warning, that Germany intends to strike her real blow, for her dream is to found an empire reaching to the Persian Gulf, that will wrest the sceptre of power from England in India and in Egypt.

It seems strange now that any one could have been blind to the meaning of the Kaiser's alliance with Turkey, and the project of the Berlin-to-Bagdad Railway. We see, however, without the shadow of a doubt that England had not prepared for a war, or else she would have been ready to go forward at the point where things might have been pushed to an early decision. But it is idle to speculate on what might have happened if England had been able to press on with vigor at the Dardanelles and to strike through the Balkans, saving Serbia and uniting with Russia in time to prevent the collapse of that ally. If it is true as one of the Sultan's henchmen declared, that it was not Turkish bravery but Allied stupidity that saved the Dardanelles, still events have shown that Destiny was working in another way.

Things came about quite naturally. The Germans and Turks thought that the British lion was asleep—else why with a Kitchener in command, one who knew the East and its opportunities, did the English not come in their ships or even across the desert to Palestine while that door was open? For at the beginning Turkey could have offered little resistance there. Surely it was a golden opportunity to destroy the Suez canal, and with it British prestige in Egypt and in India.

"It was a bit expensive, that excursion of the Turks across the desert," said an English officer. "It cost them 60,000 camels; but it came near costing us Suez."

It seemed as if representatives of all the people of the British Empire fought there at England's canal-gateway to India and the East. There were East Indians, Australians, and New Zealanders, as well as British territorials and yeomanry. Some English and French men-of-war also lent their assistance. Heavy losses were inflicted on the Turks who were put to rout with their Turkish and German leaders at Kantara, a point on the canal about thirty miles south of Port Said.

There was no doubt now that the British lion was awake. The desert must be crossed and the Turks attacked in Palestine; that northern pass to the precious canal must not be left in the hands of the enemy.

It was not the English way to depend on camel transport, however. Sir Archibald Murray, who was in command of the British forces in Egypt, decided to advance in the thorough-going Kitchener manner by laying a railroad along the Mediterranean shore from Kantara through Rafa and on up into Palestine. So the rails of a standard gauge line were laid across the desert from Cairo to Jerusalem. And the decision to proceed in this way was reached as deliberately as if the genii called upon to bridge the waste would not have to work by means of thousands of laborers to make roads, drain marshes, level embankments, and finally lay pipes to carry water along from the Nile itself across the desert. For they could no more depend upon carrying water than they could upon finding a Moses who would be able to call it

from a rock. They must take the Nile with them.
But, be it noticed, they did this in the simple, natural way of meeting a need, little dreaming that
by so doing a prophecy was being fulfilled.

Nor did General Sir Edmund Allenby, that
quiet, unpretentious commander in whom the
strength of the leader and the easy courtesy of the
English scholar and gentleman seemed perfectly
blended, have any more idea that Fate had singled
him out to lead a successful crusade and play the
part of liberator to the followers of three great
faiths than he had when he was a school-boy at
Haileybury College. It is the pride of all of England's public schools—Eton, Rugby, Harrow, and
the rest—that they so graft the fine traditions of
the past upon the sturdy stem of vigorous, well-
balanced training of mind and body, that they produce a special flowering of character which has
been the strength and glory of the British Empire. It is the boast of Haileybury that her sons
have proved particularly fit in taking up "the
white man's burden" in India and in Africa. . . .
We may note that, while still a boy at school, young
Allenby showed a love of literature. He enjoyed
the fine flavor of a book that was to his taste as
naturally as he enjoyed a game of cricket.

FIGHTERS FOR PEACE

On entering the soldier's life as a young officer of dragoons, he first saw active service in Africa at the age of twenty-three. Four years later—in 1888—he fought in Zululand, and because of his keen resourcefulness as well as his courage, he was made adjutant. In the South African War from 1899 to 1902 his gallantry and cavalry tactics which were twice mentioned by his commander in dispatches home, won him a decoration by the Government.

In the present war his division of cavalry acted as a screen to the infantry in that stubborn retreat when the Germans were making their first terrific rush on Paris, and "the contemptible little British army" of less than 200,000, hopelessly outnumbered and deluged with high-explosive shells to which they had no way of replying, fell back step by step, yielding so slowly, selling their lives so dearly, that the German onslaught was checked until Joffre could gather his forces for the stand at the Marne. It was Allenby's cavalry that, like the nimble shield of the gladiator fighting against odds, caught the deadly thrusts of the enemy, and enabled the slender columns to prolong the struggle as they did. It was also Allenby's cavalry, as General French noted in his report, that saved the heroic remnant of the British forces from destruction.

When in June, 1917, General Allenby was transferred from the Western arena and put in charge of the Palestine expedition planned by General Murray, all his gifts both as a man and as a commander were soon brought into play. During the parching heat of the summer months when nothing could go forward except plans for the offensive in the autumn, Allenby studied the situation point by point, noting the entrenchments of the enemy and the natural obstacles to be overcome. Here he proved that by careful preparation he could forestall difficulties, commanding success by a wise and prudent generalship that matched his daring gallantry when fighting against odds.

Now the Tommies who had been whiling away some of the summer days by going about with Bibles as Baedekers, trying to identify various places mentioned in church, were drawn up along a front of twenty-two miles from the sea opposite Gaza to Gamli. They faced the Turks who were strongly entrenched from Gaza to Beersheba, a distance of about thirty miles. It was General Allenby's plan to make various feint attacks to distract the enemy's attention, and then to strike boldly at Beersheba, where he knew there was an ample water supply, forcing the Turks out with a suddenness that would prevent them from damaging the famous wells.

The attack had all the effect of an unexpected pounce. The infantry was marched forward during the night, for the least movement over the parched ground raised clouds of dust that would have at once proclaimed their approach over a country covered only by a sparse growth of trees and cactus hedges. During the day, therefore, the Tommies lay hidden in the dry, pebbly ravine of a wadi, and wondered if it was from the bed of this stream that David drew his five smooth stones to slay the giant.

On the calm, moonlit night of October 30, the men prepared for a rush on a hill just south of the city, where a German machine gun section was implanted. So sudden was the onslaught that the guns were silenced and the hill carried before the eight officers and eighty men who were captured had chance to realize their plight. After a bombardment by field guns which had been placed at the right range to cut through the wire entanglements, the infantry dashed forward, screened by the pall of sand raised by the bursting shells, tore down the wire from its iron supports, and fairly swept the astonished Turks from the entrenchments they had thought well-nigh impregnable. Through the gate-way thus opened by the infantry, the Australian cavalry charged into the town from the east, completed the capture, and, by commanding the Hebron road, shut off retreat in that direction. Warehouses full of grain, which bore signs of hasty, futile attempts to destroy the stores, gave evidence to the surprise of the attack.

There was a pause for a day or two in the firing, when the Tommies with the Bibles could gather about the two circular wells of clear, pure water, and speculate freely as to which was the well dug by Abraham, which spot was the place where the patriarch received the command to sacrifice Isaac, and which stone might have been the altar where Jacob made his burnt offering to Jehovah on the journey into Egypt.

"How far is it to Dan?" asked an American Red Cross worker who chanced to recall that the phrase "from Dan to Beersheba" indicated the extent from north to south of the Hebrew territory.

"About a hundred and fifty miles," he was assured authoritatively. "Palestine is only a very

187

little larger than your Massachusetts; but no man from the Hub even, would dare to contend that this narrow strip of barren, hilly country is not more precious to the world than any other portion of the earth's surface.''

''I wonder,'' said the Red Cross man hastily, as if trying to stem the tide of an earnest discourse, ''if General Allenby will make it possible for me to take a stroll from Dan to Beersheba one of these days before I go back to our little America.''

(It may be added here by way of parenthesis that he was indeed accorded that privilege.)

But first the Tommies and the Australian light horse had the fine excitement of taking Gaza, the modern city built over the ancient town of the Philistines for which the strong man of the Israelites, Samson, showed his contempt by carrying away its gates, leaving them casually on a neighboring hill-top. The Turks had an elaborate system of trenches about the place which would have exacted a costly toll of British lives without General Allenby's strategy. By a flank attack before daylight, he succeeded in rolling back the enemy on the left step by step, until Gaza, the scene of many sieges from the time it was a possession of the Pharaoh ''who knew not Joseph,'' 1300 B. C., until it was quietly pocketed by Napoleon in 1799, was captured. Now it was once more laid in ruins, by the Turks who waited to destroy what they could not carry off. The near view, therefore, of the houses, which with their red-topped roofs and colored walls had looked rather picturesque as seen over the olive groves, was a distinct disappointment; but the Tommies found much to interest them in the captured defenses of the enemy. There were dugouts with head covers of thick palm logs thatched with sand bags, which led to shelters a dozen feet below ground. Dense hedges of cactus, in many places untouched by the bombardment, screened machine guns which would have done deadly work but for the strategy of the capture.

They were now on the open rolling Plains of Philistia, dotted with little villages enclosed within mud walls and surrounded by plantations of dates and olives. Here the cavalry in a dashing charge across a flat expanse swept by the gun fire of the enemy, succeeded in capturing Junction Station on the Jerusalem-Damascus Railroad, thus cutting in two the Turkish army, part of which had withdrawn eastward into the mountains near Jerusalem, the other section retreating north across the plain. In summing up in his official report the results of the first fortnight of his campaign, General Allenby said:

"In fifteen days our force had advanced sixty miles on its right and about forty miles on its left. It had driven a Turkish army of nine infantry divisions and one cavalry division out of a position in which it had been entrenched for six months, and had pursued it, giving battle whenever it attempted to stand, and inflicting on it losses amounting probably to nearly two-thirds of the enemy's original effectives. Over 9,000 prisoners, about 80 guns, more than 100 machine guns, and very large quantities of ammunition and other stores had been captured."

Jaffa, or Joppa as it was called in ancient times, the seaport of Jerusalem, where in the time of Solomon's glory the wealth of the world was brought, and where the famous cedars of Lebanon were sent by King Hiram of Tyre for the building of the Hebrew temple, was seized on November 17. Preparations for taking the "city set on the hill," without firing a shot which would imperil its sacred buildings were now well under way. If General Allenby had not feared to harm even the approaches to the holy city, it might have fallen

190

into his hands much sooner. As it was, he determined to close in upon it, pushing on the construction of the railway, insuring a water supply, and taking every opportunity for the landing of stores along the coast. As the main way from Jaffa to Jerusalem, the only road possible for wheeled transport, had been damaged by the Turks at several points, it was necessary to stop to make repairs before the artillery could be brought up.

They were now in the Judaean hill country, a land of steep, craggy, limestone cliffs, intersected by narrow valleys. Here to the northwest of Jerusalem, the Turks made a determined stand, fearing that communication would be cut off from the city, which they could hardly hope to hold now that the way to the sea was gone, but which as one of the holy cities of their faith, they could not bring themselves to surrender without a struggle.

Early in November, however, the Turkish officials with the Germans and Austrians began to take their flight along the Shechem road, where from the towers of the city or from the Mount of Olives, one could see a double line of dust rising for several days as a continuous stream of carts and camels made what haste they could with their heavy loads. The German commander, Falken-

hayn, marched down from Aleppo with much
bluster of efficient Kultur to pull together the demoralized army, but in a day or two he decided to
follow the dusty way along the road to Shechem.
When on December 8, General Allenby's troops
appeared in sight of Jerusalem, a wild panic seized
the Turks who still lingered weakly about the city.
Some threw away their guns as they fled; others
driven by their officers were compelled to pick up
their arms and stagger along hopelessly to the
hills.

But the inhabitants of the land—Syrians, Jews
and Arabs, who had prayed for deliverance from
the misrule of the Turk—were transported with
joy. They had had glimpses of the prosperity
of Egypt under the fair treatment of the English.
Arab traders, too, who had been delivered from
pirates blessed the strong arm of England, whose
navy policed the waters which the Turk had never
succeeded in making safe for commerce. After
four hundred years of hateful bondage to rulers
who had done nothing for the development of the
country, but had through their oppressions
robbed it of all its fertility and wealth, the Jews
also saw the dawn of a new era of freedom and
peace. There was a great running to and fro by

GENERAL SIR EDMUND ALLENBY
Commander-in-Chief of the Egyptian Expeditionary Force

girls and women calling to men who had hidden away for fear of being seized for deportation. "The Turks are running," they cried. "The day of deliverance is come!"

On December 10 the encircling of the city was complete. Welsh and English troops from the direction of Bethlehem, driving back the enemy on the east, commanded the road to Jericho, and at the same time there was an attack on the north and northwest. The city surrendered without a shot being fired within its walls.

At noon on December 11, 1917, just four hundred years after the capture of the city by the Turks in 1517, General Allenby entered Jerusalem reverently on foot, accompanied by the commanders of the French and Italian detachments, and the military attaches of France, Italy and America. At the Jaffa gate they were received by guards representing the troops of the different nations who had taken part in the campaign—England, Scotland, Ireland, Wales, Australia, New Zealand, India, France, and Italy. It was as if each in that solemn moment of triumph gave thanks in the name of his nation and of humanity for the deliverance of the city of the Prince of Peace.

There were some there who contrasted this

humble reverent procession with the pomp of the German emperor's entry in 1898, when a portion of the wall was thrown down in order that he and his imperial escort would not have to ride out of their direct path to one of the ancient gates. "Could there be a more perfect symbol of the difference between the aims of the nations who are fighting for the peace of the world, and the Germans who with their Turkish allies are struggling to preserve their autocratic power?" it was asked.

General Allenby's proclamation was a further illustration of the spirit of the conquerors who had driven out the Turk and now guaranteed to the oppressed peoples of the land the right to work out their salvation in their own way. Written in Arabic, Hebrew, English, French, Italian, Greek and Russian, it gave the following assurance:

Lest any of you be alarmed by reason of your experience at the hands of the enemy who has retired, I hereby inform you that it is my desire that every person should pursue his lawful business without fear of interruption. Furthermore, since your city is regarded with affection by the adherents of three of the great religions of mankind, and its soil has been consecrated by the prayers and pilgrimages of devout people of these religions for many centuries, therefore, I make it known to you that every sacred building, monument, holy spot, shrine, traditional site, endowment, pious bequest, or customary place of prayer of whatsoever form of the three religions will be maintained according to the existing customs and beliefs of those to whose faith they are sacred.

Guardians have been established at Bethlehem and on Rachel's tomb. The tomb at Hebron has been placed under exclusive Moslem control. The hereditary custodians at the gates of the Holy Sepulchre have been requested to take up their accustomed duties in remembrance of the magnanimous act of the Caliph Omar who protected that church.

About the famous Mosque of Omar a cordon of Mohammedan guards were stationed, beyond which only Moslems might pass.

"We are in the hands of a just man, Allah be praised!" said a tall Arab, who looked half-dervish, half-brigand, with a devout gesture. "And the name, Allenby, is a sign to the enlightened— Allah Nabi, which is to say God and Prophet. We Arabs have a prophecy: 'He who shall save Jerusalem and exalt her among the nations will enter the city on foot, and his name shall be God, the Prophet.'"

There was no difficulty in holding the "occupied territory" held in trust by Allenby's army, for the inhabitants of the land in their joyful welcome of the conquerors made it clear that to them it was liberated territory. Many of the Jewish youth who had succeeded in evading the Turks begged to be allowed to join the ranks of their deliverers, even though they knew that they would suffer dire punishment should the fortunes of war restore their former masters to power.

Preparations for a second campaign included extensive road making and completion of lines of communication. Large armies of laborers from Egypt assisted the natives in laying macadam and dirt roads throughout southern Palestine. The railway from Cairo was now double tracked and the bridge across the Nile finished, thus greatly reducing the amount of necessary re-loading and simplifying the problem of supplies.

During the winter rains and summer heat active campaigning was of course impossible, but in the autumn of 1918, General Allenby, now strongly established in the land about Jaffa and Jerusalem, was ready for a drive northward. Soon the Turks were swept from the country that had not only been feeding their army but also sending important contributions to Constantinople and Berlin.

The first advance was made along the coast. Following the plan that had succeeded so brilliantly at Beersheba, the troops moved forward under the cover of night, remaining hidden in orange and olive groves during the day. Thus the Turks from their observation posts saw no tell-tale columns of dust, and, since the Allies' air-fleet was able to sweep the sky clear of enemy planes, they could learn nothing of the movements of his army. Again as in his earlier victories, the artillery and infantry swept through the most elaborate system of defenses, opening a gate-way along the coast for the cavalry which swung around to attack from the east the villages that were already under fire from the south.

"This skilful use of the cavalry was the most effective as well as the most spectacular feature of the Palestine campaign," said one of Allenby's men. "It was a wonderful sight—the charge of the Australian light horse and the splendid Indian troopers through the coast country to the rear of the enemy. Sweeping through wadis and heavy sand as if there could be no obstacles, the cavalry rounded up the Turks before they knew that they were being attacked."

So thorough was Allenby's preparations, from the perfect organization of supply transports—carts, lorries, camel trains and donkey files—to the timing of artillery and infantry assaults in conjunction with the cavalry dash, that in little more than a fortnight the whole country north of Jerusalem to Damascus and beyond had been wrested

197

from the Turk. The submarine bases at **Haifa** and Beirut, which had menaced the whole of the eastern Mediterranean, were taken, and those harbors opened for supply ships, so that no longer would the army be compelled to depend on the railway across the desert.

The victory was complete. The Turkish forces, killed or captured, were put out of existence as armies, and all of their material of war destroyed or seized. "The whole country which I have passed through is littered with abandoned and bombed transport and ammunition depots, motors, lorries, and a large amount of rolling stock," wrote a newspaper correspondent on September 22.

Would the Turks try to gather together another army to dispatch to Aleppo to meet the two armies converging upon that point—General Marshall from his victories in Mesopotamia and General Allenby by way of Palestine? The surrender of Turkey to the Allies on October 31 put an end to all conjectures. The dominion of the Turk over unfortunate, subject peoples—Armenians, Jews, Syrians, and Arabs—was broken. A new victory had been won for peace.

And Palestine, the land which like a well-spring of spiritual comfort and inspiration has given the

198

world its greatest religious faiths, is to have an opportunity for free and untrammeled development. Those Jews who have never ceased to feel that they are exiles in other lands may return there to build up a nation about a restored Jerusalem.

Dr. John H. Finley, who as Commissioner of the American Red Cross spent some time in Palestine, gave us a picture of General Allenby, the Crusader of the World War. "An evening that I shall longest remember," he said, "was one that I spent with him at G. H. Q. over the Bible and George Adam Smith's Geography of the Holy Land. Here was a powerful, blunt-spoken, demanding warrior, with the mind of a statesman and with a smile that would bring the children of the world in a crusade behind him."

It is thus, or walking reverently with the officers of his staff into the holy city, that I like to think of the victorious commander, General Allenby, fighter for peace.

THE SPIRIT OF GARIBALDI

VICTOR EMANUEL AND HIS ARMIES

The graves burst asunder, the dead rise to aid us;
  The martyrs and heroes whose sacrifice made us,
With swords firmly grasped and with brows wreath'd with
      laurel,
  They rise now Italia's freedom to greet!
Then hasten, then haste! Onward press, brave battalions!
Fling wide to the breeze freedom's banner, Italians!
With sword and with musket press on in your ardor,
  With hearts that alone for Italia beat!
Ye aliens abandon our home-land Italian,
  The hour is at hand, shake its dust from your feet!

GARIBALDI'S WAR HYMN.

THE SPIRIT OF GARIBALDI

THERE was once a man whom the world called a dreamer, but it happened that he had the power of dreaming true. He saw his nation, Italy,—a people with the most glorious heritage of service to humanity in the realms of law, art, literature, and science—a people without a country. For the nation that had given to the world Cæsar, Marcus Aurelius, Dante, Michael Angelo, Galileo and Columbus, was an unhappy collection of little warring states ruled over by tyrants who were the puppets of a foreign power—Austria. He saw the people of Italy struggling helplessly, vainly, to win freedom to live their life and work out their destiny in their own way. The dreamer, Mazzini, of all the sons of Italy best understood the heart and the disappointed hopes of this divided nation.

"There must go forth," he said, "from the midst of the old Italy that sees itself bound hand and foot, and says 'Submission is the only wisdom!' the spirit of a young Italy that gloriously dares everything to win freedom for our native land.''

That first vision of the dreamer came to pass. There sprang up on every hand in answer to his call young, eager souls ready to live—and die if need be—for a new, liberated Italy. They were for the most part humble, unknown youths, rich only in their daring and their burning faith.

''All great national movements,'' wrote Mazzini, ''begin with the unknown mass of the people, without influence except for the faith and will that counts not difficulties.''

The lovers of liberty who gathered about the dreamer called themselves ''Young Italy,'' and this was the oath of their order:

''In the name of God and of Italy. In the name of all the martyrs of the holy Italian cause who have fallen beneath foreign and domestic tyranny. By the love I bear to the land that gave my mother birth, and will be the home of my children. By the blush that rises to my brow when I stand before the citizens of other lands, to know that I have no rights of citizenship, no country and no national flag. By the memory of our former greatness and the sense of our present degradation. By the tears of Italian mothers for their sons dead on the scaffold, in prison, or in exile. By the sufferings of the millions—I swear to dedicate myself wholly and forever to striving to constitute Italy one, free, independent, republican nation.''

The torch was lighted and Young Italy was handing it on from one cold, unthinking, or despairing group to another until the land was aflame with patriotic ardor. But everywhere there were Austrian spies ready to stamp out the glowing fires. How could the dream come true? Italy's soul was awake, but where was the sword and the mighty hand to draw it in the name of liberty?

Then there came to Mazzini a man to whom to feel and think meant to act, and he knew that the cause had found its captain. Giuseppe Garibaldi —whose name itself meant ''bold in war''— would be the mighty arm of Italy to strike the first blow in the fight for freedom.

The new leader came of humble people who had worked hard to give their bright, promising boy a good start in the world, hoping that he would make a priest. ''There is nothing like learning,'' said his father who was a sailor on a trading vessel. ''Many voyages make you love home; and many questions make you long to know what the books can teach.''

205

"There is nothing like going and doing," said the boy. "The more I read the more I hate to sit still and hear about things, instead of getting out and being a part of them. I want to be a sailor."

"You have the adventuring fancy," said his father with a sigh. "The sea has cast its spell on you." But he took the lad with him on his next voyage.

It was a great day for the boy when he first saw Rome. As he gazed upon the Eternal City his heart was strangely stirred. How wonderful was the past when Rome had been the capital of the world, and how pitiful was the present! He heard it whispered, "When will Italy have faith in the future as well as pride in the past, and boldly rise up, a free nation, with courage to cast out her foreign masters?"

That trip to Rome was the beginning of a new existence. Even while he exulted in the bold, free life of the sea, he felt a strange undercurrent of sadness. Italy, the fairest and most glorious of countries, was in chains. He had longed to fare forth and taste the spice of adventure in far-off lands; now he knew that the great adventure awaited him at home in the fight for his country's freedom.

THE SPIRIT OF GARIBALDI

As the visit to Rome was the first real event of Garibaldi's life, so the meeting with Mazzini was the second. The heart and hand of Young Italy were paired. But the time was not ripe for the crusade. Garibaldi, who had enlisted in the navy in order that he might win the sailors to the great cause, found that he was counted a conspirator against the country he longed to serve, and that his life was forfeit.

An exile from Italy, the young patriot went to South America, and was soon in the midst of the struggles of the peoples there for liberty. He gathered about him a band of his fellow country-men who had sought refuge or adventure in the new world. The cause of freedom in Uruguay and Brazil owed much to the free-lance, Garibaldi, who proved himself a veritable genius of impro-vised, guerilla warfare, and a born leader of men. His disinterested enthusiasm kindled ardor in oth-ers and won a loyal, devoted following. For four-teen years he lived and served the people's cause in South America, knowing all the time that he was preparing himself for the day when he could return with his "Legion" to fight for Italy.

That great moment came in 1848, when the spirit of democracy swelled like a mighty flood through

Europe, sweeping all before it. In France the people succeeded in overthrowing the monarchy imposed upon them after the defeat of Napoleon; and in other countries thrones trembled and the people were granted constitutions. In Italy, the King of Sardinia and Piedmont, Charles Albert, the one ruler in divided Italy who was an Italian at heart, found courage to revolt against the tyranny of Austria. To him Garibaldi appeared with his Legion of fifty picked men of those who had proved themselves in the forests and on the plains of South America. If the King looked coldly at this wild band in their scarlet shirts and slouch hats of many strange sorts, the people did not. The fame of Garibaldi's exploits had thrilled Italians at home, and in a short time thirty thousand lovers of freedom gathered under the banner of the popular hero. The sword arm of Young Italy was ready to strike.

As we pass in review the marvellous story of Garibaldi's leadership, and seek to discover the secret of the power that made him first in the battles for freedom and first in the hearts of Italians, let us recall the tribute of the admiral of the British squadron who knew him in South America: "He was the only truly disinterested individual I knew; and his courage was equalled by his great military talent.'' Always fighting against heavy odds, he went from victory to victory for a redeemed Italy, wearing his success and his power as simply as he had ever worn his red shirt and scarlet-lined poncho, which were to his followers as the helmet of Navarre in another historic struggle. There were times when Victor Emmanuel I of Italy, (son and successor of Charles Albert of Sardinia), and his minister, Cavour, whose masterly diplomacy at the helm of the ship of state carried the newly-made constitutional monarchy through many storms, fairly held their breath. Would victory and popularity make of Young Italy's General another Napoleon? But that ''Grand Old Lion of Democracy'' had only one ambition—to see Italy free. And when it was clear that the organization and discipline of the regular army fettered his powers, Victor Emmanuel said, ''Go where you like, do what you like; I feel only one regret, that I am not able to follow you.''

As he was unspoiled by fair fortune, so he was undismayed when at the turn of her wheel he was cast down. There was a dark time when Italy was not only fighting Austria, but also France, her erstwhile friend and ally, since Louis Napoleon had come to the support of the Pope in his protest against the separation of Church and State. Garibaldi, again forced into exile, lived for a while in New York, where he earned his living making tallow candles. "Each one is a taper for liberty," he used to say, his glowing brown eyes alight with the smile that won the hearts of all who knew him.

Garibaldi lived to see the greater part of his beloved Italy an independent country under one flag, but still Austria held in her grip the Trentino which put at her back the mountains that formed Italy's natural boundary and bulwark. The ancient enemy had, then, a position of military control over Lombardy and Venetia, and, indeed, of the whole "boot," since the valleys of the Trentino led into the heart of the richest industrial and commercial territory of Italy.

> Well did Nature for our State provide,
> When the bulwark of the Alps she put
> Twixt us and German fury,

sang the poet Petrarch. The claim, therefore, upon the portion of *Italia irredenta* (unredeemed Italy) known as the Trentino, is based not only upon tradition and sentiment—upon the fact that it once was Italy and still is, for the most part, Italy in feeling and speech—but also, and even more compellingly upon the necessity of self-preservation. Austria's position on the commanding peaks with control over the gateways—mountain passes and river beds—into the neighboring dominion, was a perpetual menace.

All true Italians feel that the leaders of the struggle for a free, united country—Mazzini, Garibaldi and Cavour—watch from their graves to see the completion of their work. When Cavour died Rome and Venice were still unredeemed. "They are the heart and crown of Italy," he said; "they must soon be hers. As to the Trentino and the Tyrol, that is the work of another generation." Not only to the old men of that next generation but to their stalwart sons were those words a solemn charge.

Austria was also still in possession of the eastern coast of the Adriatic—Istria and Dalmatia, which were until Napoleon meddled with the map of Europe, part of Venetia. The port of Trieste, although it had been subject to Austria for several centuries, was in population two-thirds Italian to one-third Slav. This coast land which belonged to Italy historically was, moreover, hers by the hard logic of geographical position, since the Adriatic must, for any reasonable security to the people of the peninsula, be in effect an Italian sea, as the eastern coast of Italy is entirely at the mercy of the opposite shore which possesses the natural harbors. The waters enclosed by the Istrian Peninsula and Dalmatia had been during the reign of the Cæsars a Roman lake, and at a later period the queen-lagoon of Venice. The poet d'Annunzio speaks for Italians everywhere when he says: "The name of this deep sea, where the foam on every wave is a flower of Italian glory, is and shall be forever, in the language of all nations, the Gulf of Venice."

With all the bitter memories of past wrongs and the ever-present longing to reclaim the *Italia irredenta* represented by Trieste and the Trentino, how did it happen that Italy became a member of the Triple Alliance, linking herself by treaty to her ancient enemy? Many thought Italy's moral position at the beginning of the Great War as indefensible as her geographical frontiers. "Why make an alliance one day to break it the next?" said the man in the street. "Italy is going to be sure to cast in her lot with the winning side."

The Triple Alliance was, however, from the

standpoint of Italy nothing but a league to enforce peace. At the time it was formed in 1882, she wanted above all else a chance for internal adjustment and quiet growth. According to the terms of the pact the allies were bound to come to the assistance of one of their number only in case that nation was attacked by another power. This provision for mutual defense was further qualified by Italy's stipulation that she should in no event be involved in a war with Great Britain. For Italy is linked to England by the triple bond of traditional friendship, kindred ideals, and material interest; and, should the first two links fail, her exposed position in the Mediterranean would make it suicidal for her to be party to a quarrel with the Mistress of the Seas.

At the beginning of the Great War, therefore, Italy's position was in no sense dubious. She at once declared herself neutral since her partners in the Alliance were the aggressors. Though her sympathies were all with those who were fighting for freedom and a just peace, she hesitated to fling herself headlong into the arena. For Italy has to depend on other nations for coal, iron, and food enough for her people. How could she go unprepared into war?

So much for considerations of common prudence which the guiding powers of a nation do well to weigh carefully. But what of the spirit of Garibaldi—the crusading spirit that rides against wrong and injustice without counting the cost—was that dead in the land?

As soon as the war broke out the seven grandsons of the beloved patriot foregathered from the four corners of the earth—two from America, one from a sugar plantation in Cuba, two from engineering tasks in China and in Egypt, and the two youngest from schools in Italy—to take part in the struggle. Six of them (one could not leave his railway in China until Italy entered the war) volunteered for service in the Foreign Legion in France; and a sister, Italia, who had been organizing Red Cross work in Rio de Janeiro, was also ready to serve. Let us hear what the Garibaldis themselves had to say about Italy and the war:

"I don't recall," said Colonel Giuseppe Garibaldi to a sympathetic listener as they sat at supper one January evening in his hut on the Italian Alpine front, "I don't recall anything that was actually said between us on the subject, but it seemed to be generally understood among us brothers that the shedding of some Garibaldi blood—or, better still, the sacrifice of a Garibaldi life—would be calculated to throw a great, perhaps a decisive, weight into the wavering balance in Italy, where a growing sympathy for the cause of the Allies only needed a touch to quicken it into action. Indeed I think that my father said something to that effect to the two younger boys before he sent them on to France. . . . Well— Bruno got his bullet the last week in December, and Constante fell on the 5th of January. Ezio —the youngest of the three fire-eaters—had to wait to take his bullet from the Austrians on our own front.

"The attack in which Bruno fell was one of the finest things I have ever seen. General Gouraud sent for me in person to explain why a certain system of trenches *must* be taken and held, no matter what the price. We mustered for Mass at midnight—it was Christmas or the day after, I believe—and the memory of the icicle-framed altar in the ruined, roofless church, with the flickering candles throwing just enough light to silhouette the tall form of Gouraud, who stood in front of me, will never fade from my mind.

"We went over the parapet before daybreak,

and it was in the first light of the cold winter dawn that I saw Bruno—plainly hit—straighten up from his running crouch and topple into the first of the German trenches. He was up before I could reach him, however, and I saw him clamber up on the other side, and, running without hitch or stagger, lead his men in pursuit of the fleeing enemy. . . .

"They found his body, with six bullet wounds upon it, lying where the gust from a machine-gun had caught him as he tried to climb out and lead his men beyond the last of the trenches we had been ordered to take and hold. He had charged into the trench, thrown out the enemy, and made—for whatever it was worth—the first sacrifice of his own generation of Garibaldi. We sent his body to my father and mother in Rome, where, as you will remember, his funeral was made the occasion of the most remarkable patriotic demonstration Italy has known in recent years. Constante's death a few days later only gave added impulse to the wave of popular feeling which was soon to align Italy where she belonged, in the forefront of the fight for the freedom of Europe."

Any one who has read about the Italian campaign in the Alps knows that the Garibaldi spirit

VICTOR EMMANUEL III
King of Italy

was not confined to those of the name and blood; but, from Victor Emmanuel III, patriot-king and comrade of his men on the battle front, to the faithful workers at the end of the communication lines, all were of one mind and heart. Many are the stories told of the courage and kindliness of the king, for to the people this monarch who "reigns but does not rule" is the incarnate spirit of Italy. . . . A wounded boy had been brought into a field hospital in the Trentino after a violent attack on the Italian trenches. Seeing the King who was going about as his habit was among the men awaiting the care of the surgeons, he roused himself and pointed proudly to his shattered leg. "For you, sire!" he said. "No," replied the King, looking into the boy's eyes with simple friendliness and raising his hand to the military salute, "No, my son, not for me, but for Italy!"

"At the front the King is just one of the men," it was said, "a soldier with the sense of duty of a soldier. His presence is militarily unnecessary; he attempts no leadership, but his knowledge is of much use to the Staff conducting operations. Of course what counts most is his presence, or rather his *life* at the front, as an example. He has none of the comforts of his generals, or even of many of his colonels; and this, not from any desire to pose, but because he is a soldier and not a leader. He sleeps on a camp bed even when he sleeps in a villa—these are small but not useless details— and eats at a table covered with oilcloth, taking two courses at most, like the *rancio* of his soldiers. War has changed in methods and character; the present King's grandfather could ride in the midst of his fighting soldiers and make a paint- able picture, but the present sovereign address- ing his troops would make an unimpressive figure. But there is n't a hospital at the front which he has not visited, and his relations with stricken soldiers are those of a comrade."

The spirit of Garibaldi, the crusader, who loved Italy and freedom more than life, was the spirit that animated the King and the King's armies. Can you imagine what the Alpine campaigns were like—what it meant to advance through the moun- tain passes against the fire of the enemy en- trenched on the heights? Every peak was a cita- del which nature had made well-nigh impregnable. But with the double motive of guarding the gate- ways into their beloved home-land and also re- deeming her crowning glory of mountain country from the Austrian hold, the men of the south

218

climbed on and fought on, by their ready action and gallant heroism overcoming much of the initial advantage that position gave to the enemy.

We may indicate something of what this heroic endeavor meant when we recall that before the war Italy had only one corps of trained mountain troops—the famous Alpini—while to-day there is a mighty army inured to perpendicular warfare, and all that calls for in the scaling of precipices and glaciers; in battling with avalanches and landslides as well as with cannons; in cutting tunnels and trenches through solid rock; and in building aerial tramways to swing supplies along wire rope cables from peak to peak.

Was there ever such amazing warfare as that on the gleaming heights of the Alps where each summit was an observation post or a stronghold whose artillery fire loosened avalanches from the slopes to overwhelm the assailants below, while the enemy could remain hidden in rocky caves secure from bombardment? One such fastness which the Italians actually stormed and captured included an elaborate system of gun chambers, vaults for storing ammunition and supplies, and officers' sleeping quarters with communicating passages, all safely nestled in the heart of the craggy peak. "The Austrians know how to be comfortable; perhaps that is why they are some-times caught napping," said a captain of the Alpini. "Their rock galleries were even heated and lighted by electricity."

Think of having to climb with the impedimenta of guns and blankets and lead sure-footed mules to drag cannon and carry supply-packs and hos-pital equipment. Over the teleferic railways wire baskets slide along the stout cables to help carry field guns, ammunition, food, and water to the heights, and bring back the seriously wounded one or two at a time. The men, camouflaged in white caps and coats and armed with ice-axes and alpenstocks as well as guns, frequently went for-ward on skis, by means of which they could in a moment descend from an advanced position to a sheltered place below.

The battles of the peaks have more in common with the individual fighting of olden times than anything else in modern warfare. Astonishingly small groups of men may surprise, storm, and—if all goes well—carry the points where the enemy lies in wait. There is the thrill of splendid ad-venture in an expedition where a snow-crowned summit is captured by twenty men or a difficult pass above the clouds seized by a single company aided only by three or four field guns.

Large forces of men could not work together on that battleground of heights and depths, and if they could it would be impossible to solve the problem of supplies and communication lines. "On the ordinary battle-fronts, like those of France and Russia," said Colonel Garibaldi, "it requires rather less than one man on the line of communications to maintain one man in the front-line trenches. For the whole Italian front the average is something more than two men on the communications to one in the first line; but at points in the Alps it may run up to six, or even eight or ten in bad weather." The daring fighters, then, are the apex of a pyramid which holds because it stands on a solid base of sound organization.

Sidney Low in his graphic account of "Italy in the War," gives a picture of the storming of Monte Cristallo whose sheer rock face rises some 5,000 feet above the Italian approach: "The Alpini attacked it armed with ropes, climbing-irons, and rock-drills. For a week they worked at the escalade, ignored by the Austrians, who never expected that any attempt could be made to reach them up this apparently insurmountable cliff. But the pioneers drove rings and iron pegs into the wall of rock, and from day to day mounted higher, while their comrades followed up the ladder they had made. Gradually they collected in the gullies and clefts under the summit; and then one night they stole out on the crest and rushed the Austrian garrison, too surprised and dismayed to offer more than a feeble resistance to these shouting groups of fierce foes, who seemed to have descended upon them out of the clouds.''

As the Italians won their way by faith, daring, and miracles of engineering skill from point to point in the Trentine Alps, so they advanced towards Trieste across the treacherous Isonzo River and through mountain fastnesses that blocked the way. The passage of the Isonzo north of Gorizia under the deadly fire from points of vantage all around was one of the most marvellous feats of the war. Here the engineers actually turned into another channel the main current of the river which flows at this point through a deep gorge, and constructed bridges over the shallow stream that remained. This work was all done stealthily at night and the water rediverted into its accustomed bed at daybreak. By means of the bridges so built and pontoons, the Italians swarmed over the river and dug themselves in on the lower levels of the Bainsizza Plateau, and through a surprise attack, gained a foothold on the northern edge of the rocky upland which the amazed Austrians had thought impregnable. Monte Santo was surrounded and captured a week later and the heights of Monte San Gabriele were next taken. Before the Austrians could recover and rally their forces the Italians had seized Gorizia.

As they toiled upward and onward, the conquerors were consciously building for the future. Mountain trails grew into roads where lines of concrete posts marked the ledges of the precipices, and bridges of stone or steel were built over the torrents. In many places two roads were made, one for ascent and the other for descent; and pipe-lines were run from the valleys to carry water to the crests of the mountains. The engineering feats of the Alpine fighters were no less remarkable than their triumphs at arms.

After more than two years of titanic struggle that carried them inch by inch from the lowlands to the heights fortified by Nature and surrounded by the Isonzo as by a moat, it seemed that the Italians were about to reach the rocky gateway

that opened into the castle of their hopes—Trieste
—when they were suddenly overwhelmed by disaster, and obliged to yield in a few weeks all that
they had so hardly won.

The loss of Russia to the cause of the Allies ushered in the tragic reverse. Germany shifted 100,-
000 men from the Russian border together with
some of her heaviest artillery to save Trieste for
Austria; but before launching her attack she began her offensive with intrigue. The Austrian
socialists were encouraged to fraternize with their
Italian neighbors and assure them that they would
make war against war by refusing to fight further.
The war was over in Russia, they said, and determined socialists could soon put an end to it
everywhere. When the vigilance and the morale
of the Italians were thoroughly relaxed, the Austrian front lines were suddenly withdrawn and re-
placed by German "shock troops," who broke
through the Isonzo front with a terrific rush, and,
by threatening to outflank the armies, compelled
a retreat that was at first dangerously like a rout.
The very existence of the armies seemed im-
perilled.

But at the Piave River, which had been a train-
ing-place for recruits, and so was provided with

a system of modern trenches and fortifications, the Italians rallied for a determined stand. French and British infantry were arriving to help restore the morale of the troops shaken by defeat. The line on the Piave held. As at Verdun, the watchword was "They shall not pass!" The railroads were destroyed to keep the enemy from bringing up their heavy artillery; the area between Venice and the mouth of the Piave was flooded to prevent the Austrians from crossing the river there; and the sentinel heights overlooking the Piave valley held in spite of the most desperate onslaughts. The Piave will rank with the Marne as the scene of one of the most heroic and glorious struggles of all time.

It seemed as if Fate demanded that after their hard-won successes the Italians should be further proved by the bitter discipline of defeat before tasting the fruits of victory. Then, in the summer of 1918, when the Austrians had gathered all their forces for a gigantic offensive on the Piave, Italy won as decisive a triumph as that of the Marne. The million men who had been urged forward by promises of rich stores of food just beyond the river, were put to confusion at that stream like the host of Pharaoh at the Red Sea, and the victors pursuing the defeated and demoralized army, captured men and horses by the hundred-thousand, together with vast stores of ammunition and supplies, and pressed on in triumph to Trieste and Trent. The dream of Mazzini and Garibaldi was realized; the flag of a free, united people floated over all Italy, redeemed at last. "Your victory has created a new Italy in a new Europe," declared the President of France in welcoming King Victor Emmanuel to the gathering of the nations at Paris.

The spirit of Garibaldi! "One hero have I known," wrote the French historian, Michelet, "Garibaldi, the grand of soul! Always loftier than fortune, how sublimely does his memory rise and swell towards the future!" It is, as we have seen, in the strength of that spirit which dares all in a good cause, that Italy has fought her battles of the Great War and won her splendid triumph.

"THE BIG CHIEF"

GENERAL PERSHING

"Lafayette, we are here!"

"THE BIG CHIEF"

It was one of the wisest of men who once said, "Knowledge is virtue," and while many could point out proofs of the fallacy of this saying, the life of General Pershing is a striking case where it has proved true.

"Johnny" Pershing longed for an education as most boys long for adventure. Dimly he felt that it was the way to a freer life. Starting out on that path he would find that all roads were his. As he hoed the corn on his father's little farm he dreamed of school days after the haying season should be over and the fields had yielded their harvest.

"Well, I'm off for school, Mother," he would say breathlessly, as he finished his morning chores and started on a run for the tiny frame school-house, which was yet the one place in the little frontier town of Laclede, Missouri, that commanded a view of the future and the outside world. It was not only because "Old Man Angell" might be lurking behind the door with a

229

switch to "touch up" the legs of tardy boys that he strove to be there early. He was sure that the things of the school-house could put him on the path that wound out of Laclede, out of Missouri, into the world of opportunity.

Perhaps this faith was the more remarkable because he was not by any means the "bright boy" of the school. His brother James, who was two years younger than he, was generally considered the more promising of the two. Something of the steady purpose, however, that led his Huguenot great-great-grandfather in 1724, to leave his home in Alsace, near the River Rhine, and seek his fortune as a pioneer in the new world was in that sturdy little Johnny Pershing, whose bright blue eyes, pink and white complexion, dimples, and fair, curly hair, could not conceal the fact that he was a "regular boy." Johnny knew that in Alsace his people had been called Pfoerschin, and that after they had settled in Pennsylvania it had been changed to Pershing as more American. He knew that his tall, broad-shouldered father—American pluck every inch of him—had been one whose adventurous spirit carried him to the West of golden opportunity. With only his strong body and brain as capital, he was working as boss track-layer on the North Missouri Railroad at the time he met and married Ann Elizabeth Thompson, whose people had pushed westward from the Blue Grass country. Was it Kentucky warmth and sweetness mingled with Western energy and strength that made her just the best mother that a boy ever had?

Even in those days at the village school Johnny Pershing's knowledge meant character. "Whatever he did, he did with all his might." "He was always dependable," said the people who knew the boy that grew to be the general. In the panic of '73, when the little fortune that his father had won by industry and thrift was suddenly swept away, John, then a lad of thirteen, worked hard in the fields to help support the younger children. So it was that the years passed, long seasons of work in the open that hardened his tall, vigorous body, and short terms of school that strengthened him in his resolve to get an education at any cost.

There was a time when he taught the school for negro boys in Laclede; they say that the nickname "Black Jack" Pershing, which stuck by him through his West Point years, was a souvenir of that episode in his career. Then for two years he taught the district school at Prairie Mound, nine miles away, in order that he might attend the spring term at the Kirksville Normal School.

"I am not quite sure whether I 'm headed for teaching or the law as a career," he used to say at this time, "but first and last I 'm going to get as much education as I can manage to lasso."

It seemed now as if fate were putting him to the test before throwing open the door of opportunity. The first move came in the guise of trouble; the Laclede post-office, which his father kept in connection with the village store, was robbed, and the postmaster had to make good the loss. At once young Pershing responded as waiting Destiny seemed to expect; he returned home and put in his father's hand the money he had saved to pay his way through the next school term.

Then the happy chance came his way. He read in a paper the announcement of a competitive examination for admission to West Point.

"I have no desire to enter the army," he said to his sister, "but is n't it a real opportunity to get more of an education than old Missouri can hold out?"

"It certainly seems a chance that has come your way," she replied. "Why not let the result of the examination decide for you?"

John Pershing carried off the prize by one point. "But it proved enough to point the way," he said. Despite this decision of fate, however, it was not at all clear that he wanted to be an army officer. "You know it's the education I'm after," he assured his mother, whose experiences during the Civil War in Missouri, where lawless raids and terrorism had at times held complete sway, filled her with hatred for even the thought of armies and a possible need of them.

"Of course you cannot remember that dreadful time," she said. (Pershing was born September 13, 1860.) "But, my son, every one who lived through it knows that it cannot happen again. People are wiser now, in America, at least. They will find some better way of settling their disputes."

"As soon as I have served long enough to pay Uncle Sam for my education I mean to go into something else," her son declared with conviction. "Some of the other fellows at the Point feel the same way, too. We have talked up a

233

scheme for irrigation of land in Oregon,—one of the chaps knows about it,—which needs only that to make it the most wonderful farm country in the world, and we 've planned to form a company and put it through one of these days.''

With his boyhood chum, Charlie Spurgeon, he wandered off into the woods, where they threw themselves on the ground and, looking up at the sky through the tree-tops, talked over the plans for the future.

''This country is at peace now, and it 's going to stay at peace,'' said young Pershing. ''There won't be a gun fired in the next hundred years. The army is no place for me in peace times. I 'd start as a second lieutenant and I 'd get to be a first lieutenant only when a man ahead of me died. The world is going to be too peaceful in the future to make the army look promising as a career.''

And all the time, Fate standing by, listening, was looking wise and inscrutable. But any one would have been sure that it was a kindly fate. Was the stern goddess, relaxed for the moment, even smiling to herself and saying with Puck, ''What fools these mortals be,—even the best of them,—not to be able to see and interpret their manifest destiny?"

For from the beginning of his career at West Point it was evident to every one that "Black Jack" Pershing of Missouri was a born soldier and leader of men. It was clear to General Merritt, superintendent of the academy, as he cast his keen, appraising glance over the cadets under his charge, and Pershing was given the highest rank in the battalion that it was possible for him to attain each year. It was equally plain to his classmates, who made him their president unanimously, no one else even being thought of in the moment of nomination.

We may read for ourselves some of Pershing's impressions of his cadet days in a letter that he wrote from his post in the Philippines on the occasion of the twenty-fifth reunion of his class:

The proudest days of my life, with one exception, have come to me in connection with West Point—days that stand out clear and distinct from all others. The first of these was the day I won my appointment at Trenton, Missouri, in a competitive examination with seventeen competitors. An old friend of the family happened to be in Trenton that day and, passing on the opposite side of the street, called to me and said, "John, I hear you passed with flying colors." In all seriousness, feeling the great importance of my success, I naïvely replied in a loud voice, "Yes, I did," feeling assured

that no one had ever passed such a fine examination as I
had. The next red-letter day was when I was elected president of the class of '86. To realize that a body of men for
whom I had such an affectionate regard should honor me in
this way was about all my equilibrium would stand. The
climax of days came when the makes were read out on graduation day in June, 1885. Little Eddy Gayle smiled when I
reported five minutes later with a pair of captain's chevrons
pinned on my sleeves. No honor can ever come to equal that.
I look upon it in the very small light to-day as I did then.
Some way these days stand out, and the recollection of them
has always been to me a great spur and stimulus.

In those happy days at the academy how
splendidly he showed that "Knowledge is virtue!" All that he thought and learned was immediately expressed in what he was and what he
did. Never one of the brilliant students,—at
graduation he stood thirtieth in the class of
seventy-seven,—he was yet the leader of them
all.

"Pershing was absolutely dependable," said
one of his classmates in trying to explain his
unique place in the cadet world; and another of
his fellow-students, now a brigadier-general, expressed the same thing in different words. "He
was *solid*, the sort of chap you knew you could
always count on."

"Black Jack's influence was the more remarkable because he was not one of the leaders in the

class-room,'' said another officer, who had known
Pershing at the academy. ''It is a proof that it
is character that counts, and that *knowing*
does n't signify until it gets over into *being*.
You felt what he was by the way he held himself,
with a dignity that was all power, never stiffness
or pride. You could tell by the way he sat his
horse that he would be master of himself and any
situation in which he was placed.''

''His face was an index to the man,'' said still
another member of his class. ''You could read
in the determined jaw, the clear-eyed, direct
look, and the smile that always seemed just back
of his keen glance, that he would be strict, but
always fair—a truly human leader, never a machine disciplinarian.''

It may have been necessary in order to satisfy
this young man, who felt that the army in peace
times was no place for one who had ambition to
be up and doing, that he should have been singled
out for the busiest posts and the hardest tasks
in the service. With the exception of four years
at Lincoln, Nebraska, where he was instructor in
military science at the university, and one year as
assistant professor of tactics at West Point, he
was always in the field. Perhaps watchful Des-

tiny, noticing that he was seizing the chance offered by his residence at the University of Nebraska to realize his early ambition to study law, felt that even yet her general might succeed in giving her the slip if she failed to keep him busy enough.

The second lieutenant, fresh from his success at West Point, was at once put to the test, and the actual training of the "Big Chief" began in the Apache country of New Mexico. George MacAdam in his "Life of General Pershing" says:

Physically, the country in which Pershing got his first schooling as a regular Army officer is identical with the country in which thirty years later he led that great man-hunt (for "Villa, dead or alive,")—the same baffling net-work of mountains, the same maze of seamed and rock-strewn cañons, the same blistering stretches of alkali sands, the same broiling sun by day and nipping air by night, the same cruel scarcity of water, the same elusive trails.

The Apache Indian is the unique product of a hard struggle with this unfriendly environment. Fleet of foot, he can run an astonishing distance over the alkali wastes or through the mountain trails without rest; thriving on hardship, he can subsist for days on field mice and the juice of the giant cactus; skilled in nature's camouflage, he can completely hide himself through a clever employment of grass, brush, and feathers; he was indeed an enemy to be reckoned with. When Lieutenant Pershing began his course in the new school of experience, his fellows had just emerged in triumph from the advanced problems presented by the hunt for Geronimo, the fierce Apache chief who had been finally brought to bay in September, 1886, by General Miles's relentless pursuit through New Mexico, Arizona, and northern Mexico with different detachments and commands for five months. And we read in the reports of General Miles that among the men trained to scouting and hard pursuit of marauders—white desperadoes as well as redskins—in that wild, lawless country, the newly-tried second lieutenant had won special mention.

One citation may serve to illustrate the way in which his sterling dependability was winning recognition. He had brought in his troop, plus a pack train, from a record march of one hundred and forty miles in forty-six hours, earning honorable mention from General Miles, who made particular note of the fact that he had reported "with every man and animal in good condition."

The character that found expression in his faithfulness to every detail of his charge was felt alike by the men in the ranks and the officers in command. One of the officers, who was Pershing's senior by six years of service among the Indians, said of him: "Of course one did n't ordinarily look to the striplings fresh in the field for suggestions and opinions. But there was something about Pershing that made him an exception. One found oneself turning to him instinctively with a "What do you think about it, Pershing?' And when he talked, people listened because he had a way of going to the meat of a question in a few words."

One day word came of trouble on the Zuñi Reservation. Some cowboys had been caught by the Indians driving off a number of their horses, and in the struggle that ensued three of the outraged Zuñis had been shot. The desperadoes had then taken refuge in a cabin, where they were besieged by the thoroughly aroused tribe. Colonel Carr, then in command of the Sixth Cavalry at Fort Wingate, turned to Lieutenant Pershing in this emergency.

"Of course they don't deserve help," he said grimly. "But it 's a case of putting out a fire instead of arguing about it."

When the young officer arrived with ten of his

GENERAL JOHN JOSEPH PERSHING
Commander-in-Chief of the American Expeditionary Forces

men at the scene of the trouble, he found a hundred and fifty of the incensed Zuñis drawn up about the cabin, trying to decide on the particular form their vengeance should take. Pershing went up at once to the chief. His words were few, but effective, and the Indian, looking into his eyes, read something there that spoke without the need of an interpreter.

"Will you trust me to bring out the men and take them away for trial?" he asked. "Will you take my word that justice shall be done?"

The old chief, with his eyes still fixed piercingly on the face of the tall, square-jawed young cavalryman, grunted his assent. Then Pershing forced open the door of the cabin, and faced the outlaws as if he did not even see the rifles that covered him.

"You will give up your arms and come with me quietly," he said. "I will guarantee that the Indians do not touch you." There was a brief flourish and bluster of profane threats, but somehow the direct look of the young officer put them to silence and, perhaps, to shame. Sullenly they gave themselves up, because on second thought they could hardly defy their rescuer. And the second lieutenant who had settled the unpleasant affair without bloodshed was "highly commended for his discretion."

During seven years, while he was gaining experience and winning golden opinions, Pershing served without any promotion in rank. In 1893 he became first lieutenant of a troop of negro cavalry, and the nickname "Black Jack," getting by this chance fresh point, stuck to him throughout his career. When the war with Spain broke out, he was filling the position of instructor of tactics at West Point, but he immediately applied for his old command of the Tenth Cavalry, and his "black riders" earned an enviable reputation at San Juan and at Santiago de Cuba. General Baldwin, under whom Pershing served, said of him, "I have been in many fights through the Civil War, but Captain Pershing is the coolest man under fire that I ever saw in my life." He was recommended for brevet commissions "for personal gallantry, untiring energy, and faithfulness," in the battle of El Cany winning his captaincy through distinguished valor in action.

It was thought that his courage, coupled with the qualities of faithfulness and discretion, made Captain Pershing ideally adapted to meeting the problems that America had suddenly inherited

with her island possessions in the Pacific. So he
was assigned to the task of subduing the Moros,
the fierce little Malay Mohammedans whose Vik-
ing-like raids had long been the terror of the civilized inhabitants of the Philippines. Now the
United States undertook to cope with a situation
that the Spaniards had never succeeded in handling.

The last chapter of the Moro campaign was
exceedingly dramatic. A band of Moros, entrenched in the crater of an extinct volcano on the
Island of Jolo, were defying every attempt to
put an end to their forays. The people of the
surrounding country were always in danger of
an eruption of these fire-eating fanatics, who descended upon them without warning, breathing
out threatenings and slaughter, for to them the
plundering of infidels was always a "holy war."

"Here is a new version of Mohammed and the
mountain," said Captain Pershing. "Because it
does too much coming to us we must go to it, and
after it. We must put that volcano out of business."

Accordingly he set out through the jungles,
fighting ambushed Moros every step of the way,
until he came with his picked regulars to the

243

foot of the mountain. Here they formed a cordon and cleverly fortified against attack from above, waited for the besieged Malays to come out. Again and again some daring ones, who tried to rush through the relentless cordon to the shelter of the jungle, ran to their death. Then on Christmas day, 1911, four hundred of the fierce, little brown fighters marched in a tragic procession down the mountainside and surrendered.

The final and decisive triumph came in June, 1913, at the battle of Bagsag, where the fanatics were gathered for a last stand, in the name of their prophet, against the Christian usurpers from far-away America. After that their subjugation was complete, for Pershing's peaceful victories were as remarkable as his successes in the field. He learned the language of the Moros, and tried painstakingly to get their point of view. His kindness and absolute fairness at last bore fruit, and his work as an administrator was a signal success. The Sultan of Oato even offered to bestow upon him his young son as a convincing token of his regard, at the same time conferring on him the full rights of hereditary ruler of the Moros, with the added authority of a Mohammedan judge—an honor never before entrusted to one of an alien religion.

As early as 1903 his brilliant successes in the Philippine campaigns and his marked qualities of leadership moved General Davis to write at length to Washington, recommending that he be made brigadier-general, for under the existing regulations there was no way of passing him over the heads of senior captains to a colonelcy. In that same year the distinction came to him of special mention in President Roosevelt's annual message to Congress, where, in asking that a law be passed making a reasonable promotion for distinguished ability possible, the President said: "When a man renders such service as Captain Pershing rendered last spring in the Moro campaign, it ought to be possible to reward him without at once jumping him to the grade of brigadier-general."

For three years President Roosevelt waited for Congress to take this action, and then, taking the bull by the horns, he made him a brigadier-general over 862 officers of senior grade, the most spectacular jump ever recorded in the annals of the army.

It was openly said—and the bitterness of the

slander all but poisoned the new general's happy triumph—that he had won the promotion through the influence of his father-in-law, Senator Warren of Wyoming, who was at that time a member of the Senate Committee on Military Affairs. But in 1903 when President Roosevelt made his recommendation to Congress, Pershing had not even met Miss Frances Warren, who was destined to become his wife. It is said, however, that she was sitting in the gallery when the President's message was read, and that she remarked to a companion, "I should really like to see the captain who has been able to win such a commendation."

It was not long before Miss Warren had her wish. He came, she saw, and he conquered! Most opportunely, it seemed to them then, he received the appointment of military attaché to Japan. Tokio would be an ideal place for a honeymoon; and if hard work could ever lay claim to a holiday, surely Captain Pershing was entitled to one now. But hardly had they reached the Land of the Cherry Blossom before the bridegroom was ordered to Manchuria as military observer of the battles between little Nippon and the Russian bear. And the report he forwarded to the War Department, it may be mentioned, was considered one of the most clear-cut and valuable documents of the sort ever sent in from the field.

The only way that Pershing could clear himself of the imputation of having won his promotion through favoritism was by seeking more and harder tasks. Back in the Philippines again, he brought, as we have seen, the Moro campaign to a successful conclusion in 1913, and served as commander of the Department of Mindañao and governor of the Moro Province. In December, 1913, Major-General Bell wrote in his report to Congress: "I know of nothing connected with the service of General Pershing and the army in Mindañao during the past three years which merits anything but praise."

In the summer of 1915 General Pershing was sent to the Mexican border. And now it seemed as if fate was putting both the man and the soldier to the supreme test. Was the experience of the years all available in power to meet the problems of existence? Could he face grief and defeat unshaken? In August, when the commander went to El Paso, he left his wife and children at the Presidio in San Francisco, while he was looking for suitable quarters for them in Texas. Then in a moment came the tragedy. A fire, which swept the military post near the Golden Gate, carried away Mrs. Pershing and their three daughters, all the family except the little son, Warren, whom the servants had succeeded in rescuing from the flames.

Would the Big Chief, as the men affectionately called the general, be able to meet this ordeal? "He met it like a soldier," wrote a young officer in a letter home. "I find myself thinking as I see him going about, unbowed, unconquerable, of the picture Walt Whitman drew of a soldier-soul, victorious in defeat.

'Yet mid the ruins Pride Colossal stands unshaken to the last, Endurance, resolution to the last.' "

The soul of the general, who naturally longed to push his campaign through to definite success, was also sorely tried by the restraining orders from Washington. For months he had to remain virtually inactive, carrying out the policy of "watchful waiting" while keeping his powder dry and his lines of communication intact. Perhaps the way in which he stood this test without impatience, complaint, or criticism, showed his finely tempered strength even better than his coolness in action. The general waited for orders from his commander-in-chief with the completely disciplined will of the true soldier.

When President Wilson, from among all the American commanders, chose General Pershing to lead the United States troops in the World War, he must have weighed carefully and prayerfully all the qualities of the man. American manhood was to be tried as never before. What a task it was to take the untrained boys of our free, peaceful, and prosperous republic and make them into a disciplined army nerved to endure the hardships and the horrors of the most terrible of all wars! What a responsibility to plan wisely when so many precious lives were at stake!

The way in which General Pershing took up his work of planning, providing, and organizing, and at once found his place as part of the great army of freedom proved the measure of the man.

"I shall never forget," said General Foch, "that tragic day in March when, stirred by a generous impulse, you came and placed at my disposition the entire resources of your army. The success won in the hard fighting by the American troops is the consequence of the excellent conception, command, and organization of the American general staff and the will to win of the American soldiers.''

''You have come, God bless you!'' said Marshal Joffre, in welcoming General Pershing, who had just stepped from the special train that brought him to Paris. A man, standing near, said: ''I never want to see anything finer than the meeting of those two. Both hands of each went out to the other. Then they stood a minute, face to face, perfect understanding without the need of words.''

A French captain on duty in America tried to explain what the coming of Pershing's troops to the firing-line had meant:

''Your general—he seems to us the type of your strong, straight, fearless country,'' he said. ''When we got to know your men we saw that they all had the same spirit. Can you understand how we watched to see how the Americans would go over the top—how they would hold out under fire? We could not believe that such free, happy boys, who had not been trained to war, could stand the terrible test of battle as it is to-day. The Germans had said, 'The Americans cannot fight; they have money—that is all.

They can send food and munitions, which we can send to the bottom on the way over. Americans are all for peace and profit; they will never fight!' "

Then he went on to describe the way in which the United States troops were placed for their first trial between seasoned Tommies and poilus, who, it was hoped, would manage to carry them through.

"I was there!" finished the captain, dramatically. "For once we were thinking of something besides Fritz and his tricks. We were watching the Americans under fire for the first time. And we found out they could fight! Our men did not have to lead the way; no, it was all that they could do to hold the Sammies back when the moment came for a pause and a new start. They were fine, gallant lads—so gay and so brave! We looked at each other, we French, and said, 'Well, America 's in!' "

One likes to picture the great moment when Pershing stood before the tomb of Lafayette. Stepping forward to place a wreath there he spoke only these words, "Lafayette, we are here!" That was all there was to say for his American troops; for the rest they would prove themselves in action. And how they proved themselves at Chateau-Thierry, at Saint Mihiel, at the Meuse and at Verdun, history must tell the story.

"An important part of our victory," said General Foch, "is due to the action undertaken and well carried through by the American army upon the two banks of the Meuse. For the last two months the Americans have fought in a most difficult region a fierce and ceaseless battle. The complete triumph of this struggle is due to the fine qualities displayed by all. The name 'Meuse' may be inscribed proudly upon the American flag."

When General Pershing spoke of his soldiers it was not so much their achievements as their character that moved him.

"What we have done must speak for itself," he said, "but when I think of the behavior of our men fighting here in a foreign land; of the disciplined cheerfulness with which they have faced discomforts; of the determination with which they have confronted difficulties; and of the splendid dash with which they have met the enemy, first in trench warfare and then in open battle—I cannot speak what is in my mind, because my

emotions of gratitude are so great they keep
me from speaking of these things."

Like general, like men. It is good to think
that the Commander of the American Expeditionary Forces seemed to the Allies the perfect
type of the American soldier. It is also good to
think that it was because the men in the trenches,
no less than the Big Chief, proved themselves in
terms of character—by their

> "clear-grained human worth
> And brave old wisdom of sincerity."

Thanksgiving Day, 1918, was a memorable occasion with the American Army in France.
From the vantage-ground of victory all looked
back in thankfulness that they had passed
through the fiery trials of the past months of battle, and all looked forward in confidence to a better order as the result of their devotion and sacrifice. It seemed as if General Pershing was inspired to voice in that moment something of the
inarticulate longing of all hearts.

One of those present recalled the words of a
Frenchwoman with whom the general was quar-
tered for a short time in one of the little towns,

"He look like ze statue carve out of stone, but he speak to me like a good neighbor who live long next door."

He stood there facing his troops, the ideal soldier figure, lithe, erect, indomitable. His face bore its usual expression of serene strength; but if one could not read his emotion there, all none the less surely felt it.

"May we give thanks that unselfish service has given us new vision," he said in conclusion, "that we are able to return to our firesides and our country with higher aims and a firmer purpose. . . . Our nation awaits the return of its soldiers, believing in the stability of character that has come from self-discipline and self-sacrifice. Confident of the new power that the stern school of war and discipline has brought to each of us, American mothers await with loving hearts their gallant sons. Great cause have we to thank God for trials successfully met and victories won. Still more should we thank Him for the golden future with its wealth of opportunity and its hope of a permanent universal peace."

THE CHIVALRY OF THE SEA

ADMIRAL BEATTY

"Over the warring waters, beneath the wandering skies,
The heart of Britain roameth, the Chivalry of the sea,
Where Spring never bringeth a flower, nor bird singeth in a
    tree;
Far, afar, O beloved, beyond the sight of our eyes,
Over the warring waters, beneath the stormy skies."

ROBERT BRIDGES.

THE CHIVALRY OF THE SEA

Have you seen the something in the eyes of a man who looks much upon the sea and who loves with all his being

"His sea in no wonder the same—his sea and the same
through each wonder:
His sea as she rages or stills—"

that is akin to the unfathomed deep? He is perhaps only a rough, unlettered seaman, but in his brooding face you feel the wisdom and patience of one who has known the power of eternal things.

Have you felt the something of mystery, of haunting charm, and of strength in the soul of a great nation that loves the sea? England and her mighty sea-lover—the romance of it! England, the patient sea-wife, sending her sons across the waves to strike root in new lands— the home-making power of it! One cannot rightly understand what great fleets and the chivalry of the sea may mean until he feels that the passionate love for the ocean that surrounds her isle is the very heart of England.

FIGHTERS FOR PEACE

A fleet is not built in a day or in a year and a day. The patience of centuries must season and temper it. They tell us that Alfred the Great was the founder of the Royal Navy. Just as he saw that the warring factions within the nation needed the guiding hand of a strong leader, so he also realized that the sea wall that separated their country from foes abroad could not be trusted unless it was manned by a fleet of guardian ships under the King's control. The English had always been a sea-faring people; adventure upon the waves was their life. King Alfred but chose and strengthened for the nation's defense some of the hearts of oak that had already known the sea. The navy, then, was a selected, perfected part of England's ships, all of which might be counted to rally at the country's call in time of need. When Spain put forth all her proud strength in the Invincible Armada to humble England, the Royal Navy comprised only twenty-eight ships. The sole advantage that the English possessed lay in the skill and courage of the seamen who were used to riding upon stormy seas and braving the wrath of winds and waves. All the towns of the realm who were called upon to provide ships to reinforce the navy came loyally to the defense of their land. London town when asked for fifteen sails sent double that number; and the nobles provided in addition some forty-three ships at their own expense. Indeed it seemed that, from Lord Howard, admiral of the navy, to the humblest fisherman along shore, all England was putting forth her strength on the sea she knew and trusted.

We know how the daring of Sir Francis Drake and his gallant rovers, aided by tempest and storm-lashed waves, defeated the mighty Armada. Surely England's sea and England's sons might be counted on always to rise up together against all threatening foes. Devonshire men, especially, cherished the memory of Drake and his drum, which, when dying in a distant land, he sent to be hung on the sea wall at home. And they say that in time of danger a staunch British hand needs but to strike that drum to call the spirit of Drake and the souls of all true men that have ever loved and fought for England to her rescue. It was Drake's spirit that guided Nelson, they said, to his victory at Trafalgar; and Drake's spirit was still alive in the Admiral of the Grand Fleet that held the gates of the North Sea against the dreadnoughts and destroyers of Germany.

Do you know the chantey of the Devonshiremen? It rings with the spirit of daring, sea-faring hearts of oak that know but one service, that of the sea-swept isle, and but one standard, "England expects every man to do his duty."

"Drake he's in his hammock till the great Armadas come,
   (Capten, art tha sleepin' there below?)
Slung atween the round shot, listenin' for the drum,
   An' dreamin' arl the time o' Plymouth Hoe.
Call him on the deep sea, call him up the Sound,
   Call him when ye sail to meet the foe;
Where the old trade's plyin' an' the old flag flyin',
   They shall find him ware an' wakin', as they found him
     long ago!"

Let us see how the unconquerable spirit of the past that "starts from every wave" has wrought and fought for England on the seas in the Great War. First of all there was the Grand Fleet, England's mightiest and swiftest men-of-war with their attendant cruisers, destroyers, and submarines. This was gathered in the North Sea to challenge the German Over Seas Fleet at the moment it made the attempt to leave its fortified, land-locked harbors. How well it did its work is shown by the successful "containing" of the super-dreadnoughts and destroyers of the second navy in the world during the entire period of the war, so that at the end they were obliged to give themselves up, untried, unscarred, unhonored—idle, impotent giants.

"If they were Yankee ships you had been trying to bottle up, I dare swear that some of our raiders would have slipped by," boasted an American ensign. "You can't tell me that you could have kept the three hundred miles of dark, fog-wrapt, or stormy sea between Scotland and Norway every night for three and a half years so that we wouldn't have been able to have things our way now and again."

The British bluejacket grinned with friendly tolerance. "We keep on the job, sir," he said with modest brevity.

The American looked at the lean, weathered face of the old sea-dog with keen, admiring appreciation. "I guess you've been in a pretty good school," he said, as he recalled how an officer on one of the destroyers of the Grand Fleet had described the hardships of cruising at top speed through the short, choppy waves of the North Sea:

261

"We never steam less than twenty knots," he had said, "and you can picture what that means when there is even a small sea running. Choked with oil-fuel smoke, slashed with icy spray, soaked to the skin, freezing, and utterly miserable, the spirit of our men is simply beyond all praise."

In the long winter nights when the haze veiled friends and foes alike in a wet grayness, dark patches moving through the mist were challenged by every sense and every instinct at highest pitch of alertness. This is the way an engagement with some German light cruisers who attempted to "cut some capers" in the North Sea was described by an eye-witness: "When the range reached the 2,000 yards mark the forward six-inch gun of the British cruiser spoke, a short, sharp crack that hurt the ears, followed by the duller boom of the bursting of shell. It was the fitting beginning for the inferno of noise that immediately followed. It was a fight in the dark, where no man could see how his brother fared and when it was only just possible to make out the opposing gray shadow, and hammer, hammer, hammer at it till the eyes ached and smarted, and the breath whistled through lips parched with the acrid, stifling fumes of picric acid."

THE CHIVALRY OF THE SEA

The raids attempted early in the war on the north-east coast of England by some detached and too-daring swift cruisers were so severely punished that before long all Germany's fierce seadogs of war were "contained" in their harbor-kennels. Two such sallies made by fleet, furtive cruisers, which scattered mines, and fired at long range through screening fog upon unprotected coast towns, without any excuse of military advantage, slaughtering women and children and wrecking houses and churches before they scuttled ignominiously back to the shelter of their port, were considered triumphs of "frightfulness"; but the third proved so costly that only minor excursions of smaller craft were afterwards attempted. When Admiral Beatty's patrolling fleet sighted on January 24, 1915, a squadron of cruisers and destroyers about thirty miles from the English coast, there was such swift pursuit and punishment as left little doubt that Britannia still ruled the waves.

"On land we can beat you, but here, no," said one of the miserable survivors of the *Blücher*, a 15,000-ton ship that did not succeed in getting her wounded hulk to the shelter of the shore guns, as did some of the more fortunate raiders. The

263

following extract from the account of one of the
German officers rescued from the *Blücher* gives
a lurid picture of warfare at sea under modern
conditions:

The shells came thick and fast, with a horrible droning
hum. At once they did terrible execution. The electric plant
was soon destroyed, and the ship plunged in a darkness that
could be felt. "You could not see your hand before your
nose," said one. Down below decks there was horror and confusion, mingled with gasping shouts and moans, as the shells
plunged through the decks. It was only later, when the range
shortened, that they tore holes in the ship's sides and raked
her decks. At first they came dropping from the skies. They
penetrated the decks. They bored their way even to the
stokehold. The coal in the bunkers was set on fire. Since
the bunkers were half empty, the fire burned merrily. In the
engine-room a shell licked up the oil and sprayed it around in
flames of blue and green, scarring its victims and blazing
where it fell. Men huddled together in dark compartments,
but the shells sought them out, and there death had a rich
harvest.

The terrific air-pressure resulting from explosion in a confined space, left a deep impression on the minds of the men.
The air, it would seem, roars through every opening and
tears its way through every weak spot. All loose and inse-
cure fittings are transformed into moving instruments of destruction. Open doors bang to and jamb, and closed iron doors
bend outward like tinplates, and through it all the bodies of
men are whirled about like dead leaves in a winter blast. . . .
If it was appalling below deck, it was more appalling above.
"It was one continuous explosion," said a gunner. The ship
heeled over as the broadsides struck her, then righted herself,
rocking like a cradle. Gun crews were so destroyed that

stokers had to be requisitioned to carry ammunition. Men lay flat for safety. The decks presented a tangled mass of scrap iron.

For the entire period of the war the vaunted High Seas Fleet remained paralyzed in canals and harbors. Only once did it venture out for a trial of strength. On the afternoon of May 31, 1916, a large body of German war-cruisers and destroyers appeared beyond the shore defenses, to offer battle in open sea to Admiral Beatty's squadron of cruisers, hoping to lure it away from the rest of the Grand Fleet, perhaps to its destruction in the mine-strewn waters within range of the mighty guns from the shore. First, the Germans sent out their battle-cruisers and a number of submarines, by whose activities they hoped to so confuse and perplex the advance guard of the Grand Fleet that even if it did not venture within the fatal area of mines, the whole German fleet would have chance to appear in force and annihilate it before rescue could come from the battle-ships under Jellicoe.

A strange, unearthly conflict it was, between vessels lurking in haze and smoke-screens at extreme range to escape torpedoes and, while running at top speed, striking out at each other in darkness or in sudden flashes of light through the smoke-charged mist. Destroyers dashed back and forth, now charging, now withdrawing. Now and then lurid flares of licking flames outlined for a few minutes the looming form of one of the ghostly combatants mast high, before the mist once more swallowed it up.

"I never expect to know a more thrilling moment," said one of the officers of the Grand Fleet, "than that when our far-flung battle-line took shape—miles of it shrouded in mist—as our ships found themselves with drill-like precision, and began belching out sheets of flame and clouds of smoke."

So it was that the Battle of Jutland proceeded, and but for adverse weather conditions that brought shrouding darkness early that May evening, Admiral Jellicoe might have succeeded in annihilating the German fleet.

As it was, proceeding with the greatest care, since it was difficult to distinguish between his own ships and those of the enemy, he saw the prize melt away in the heavy North Sea haze and veiling smoke-screens. Then under the pall of darkness the shattered and crippled German vessels picked their way through

their mine fields to the haven of their guarded
ports.

"If only we had not been so unlucky in the
weather!" said one of the British officers, rue-
fully. "But in that case perhaps there would
have been no Battle of Jutland, because it's a
safe guess that the Huns would never have put
out."

At first the Germans loudly proclaimed a triumph over the Grand Fleet; but afterwards, when
they could show no fruits of victory in freedom
from the blockade, when month after month their
ships remained sealed up in their harbors, the
self-evident facts silenced their boasts. As one
neutral newspaper put it: "It would seem that
the Germans might think it rather absurd to hail
their Kaiser as "Admiral of the Atlantic" before
he has a single ship afloat there. The German
Navy is undoubtedly still a navy in jail. It may
assault its keeper now and then with great fury,
but it remains in jail, nevertheless."

After the Battle of Jutland the admiral of the
fleet was made First Sea Lord of the Admiralty.
This put him in control of the policy and the
strategy of all the British naval operations everywhere. Some one has said of Sir John Jel-

licoe that he has the "candor of the sea," the large freedom of men who are used to wide spaces, and days and nights alone on the restless waters under the eternal sky.

"He has the spirit of Sir Francis Drake!" whispered the seamen.

"Not so," said a young officer, who knew the tales of Devonshire and a few of the fancies of the poets, "Drake's man is the other, the younger one, with the flashing eyes and 'the soul like a North Sea storm'."

That was Sir David Beatty, who had commanded the cruiser squadron at the Battle of Jutland, and who succeeded Jellicoe as Admiral. After that engagement he wrote in a letter, "We will be ready for them next time. Please God it will come soon." At the same time the commander-in-chief was writing of him, "Sir David Beatty showed all his fine qualities of gallant leadership, firm determination, and correct strategical insight."

"Yes," said an American officer, "I was one of those who had the privilege of serving during the last year of the war under Admiral Beatty, and one may well say in the fashion of your poet,

THE CHIVALRY OF THE SEA

Noyes, that he had the power and sweep 'of a North Sea storm,' but he also had at the same time the large wisdom of a Foch in his grasp of all of the many moves in the complex game he played, and in his masterly strategy.''

But the ships of the Grand Fleet were the aristocrats, the powerful chieftains of England's mariner hosts. What of the humble cargo boats, the trawlers, the rank and file of those from yacht to fishing-smack who held the net of the blockade from Ireland to the Mediterranean? For, as in the days of Elizabeth and the Armada, when the Royal Navy was supplemented by the boats of the people, so now all the men and all the ships of this great seafaring nation had rallied to the service of their country. How the lines of Kipling made one feel the pathos and the glory of these storm-tossed tramp boats!

> "In Lowestoft a boat was laid,
>   Mark well what I do say!
> And she was built for the herring trade,
>   But she has gone a-rovin', a-rovin,' a-rovin',
>   The Lord knows where!
>
> They gave her Government coal to burn,
> And a Q. F. gun at bow and stern,
> And sent her out a-rovin', etc.

269

FIGHTERS FOR PEACE

Her skipper was mate of a bucko ship,
Which always killed one man per trip,
So he is used to rovin', etc.

  •   •   •   •   •   •   •   •   •

Her cook was chef of the Lost Dogs' Home,
  Mark well what I do say!
And I'm sorry for Fritz when they all come
  A-rovin', a-rovin', a-roarin' and a-rovin',
  Round the North Sea rovin',
  The Lord knows where!"

It was a game with grim rules and lonely vigils, the keeping of the blockade. For a month or more at a time each boat held its watch, weaving in and out through fog and gale, not knowing at what moment a mine or the torpedo of a submarine might put a sudden end to its service.

"Out at sea and working on deck for at least twenty hours," said a fisherman, "wet through to the skin, then below for two hours' sleep. Then come on deck for another twenty hours, and keep on doing that for a month, Blow high, blow low, rain, hail, or snow, mines or submarines, we have to go through it."

"We have just crawled into port again," wrote a skipper; "what weather it has been—nothing but gales, rain, and snow, with rough seas. The strictest look-out must be kept at all times, as, with the rough seas that are going now, a submarine's periscope takes a bit of spotting, likewise a floating mine. The watchers hang on to the rigging in blinding rain, with seas drenching over them for four hours at a time, peering into the darkness.''

And as for the trawlers: "See that wire rope?" said Kipling's "common sweeper." "Well, it leads through that lead to the ship which you're sweepin' *with*. She makes her end fast and you make yourn. Then you sweep together at whichever depth you've agreed upon between you by means of that arrangement there which regulates the depth. They give you a glass sort o' thing for keepin' your distance from the other ship, but *that's* not wanted if you know each other. Well, then, you sweep, as the sayin' is. There's nothin' *in* it. You sweep till this wire rope fouls the bloomin' mines. Then you go on till they appear at the surface, so to say, and then you explodes them by means of shootin' at 'em with that rifle in the galley there. There's nothin' in sweepin' more than that."

"And if you hit a mine?" he was asked.

"You go up—but you hadn't ought to hit 'em, if you're careful. The thing is to get hold of

271

the first mine all right, and then you go on to the next, and so on, in a way o' speakin.''

"And you can fish, too, 'tween times,'' put in a voice from the next boat. Mr. Kipling's description in "The Fringes of the Fleet" makes one feel that all the Mark Tapleys of the United Kingdom had taken to trawling. But after reading about the men on patrol duty manning the destroyers that will "neither rise up and fly clear like the hydroplanes, nor dive and be done with it like the submarines, but imitate the vices of both,'' you think there is even some surplus optimism on duty there:

"Where the East wind is brewed fresh and fresh every morning,
   And the balmy night-breezes blow straight from the Pole,
I heard a destroyer sing: "What an enjoyable life does one
      lead on the North Sea Patrol!

   .   .   .   .

We warn from disaster the mercantile master
Who takes in high dudgeon our life-saving rôle,
For every one's grousing at docking and dowsing
   The marks and the lights on the North Sea Patrol."

What epic adventures filled the days and nights of the mariners of England, whose task it was to bridge the seas for the ships carrying coal and iron to France and Italy, food and munitions to

ADMIRAL SIR DAVID BEATTY
Commander of the Grand Fleet of the British Navy

all of the Allies, troops from Canada, India, Australia, and America to the battle-line in France, besides armies and supplies to other scenes of action, Gallipoli, Greece, Suez, Palestine, Mesopotamia. Had it not been for the mastery of the seas, the Germans must have become masters of the world.

"May not the great might of England's navy become a menace to the freedom of other nations and the peace of the world?" it is sometimes asked. "May not the navalism of Great Britain prove as much a threat as the militarism of Germany?"

Let the facts of the case make reply. As the people of England are what they are by virtue of their intimate association with the sea, so the government of Great Britain, the most complete democracy in the world, may be said to be the outgrowth of her sea-power. The sea breathes the spirit of freedom; seapower makes for defense and independence, not aggression. Only when it might be used as an adjunct to a powerful army could it become a threat to the liberty of other peoples.

America certainly owes much to the seapower of Britain. Admiral Mahan, in an article which appeared in the "Scientific American," stated the matter very clearly:

"Why do English innate political conceptions of popular representative government, of the balance of law and liberty, prevail in North America from the Arctic Circle to the Gulf of Mexico, from the Atlantic to the Pacific? Because the command of the sea at the decisive era belonged to Great Britain."

Turning now to the testimony of the Norwegian, Nils Sten, we read:

"I have traveled by German steamers nearly all over the world, but never heard (until August, 1914) a German officer complain of England's naval supremacy . . . For the last 100 years Norway has been England's greatest competitor on the sea. When has Norway had reason to complain of England's jealousy or English supremacy? In all the harbors of the world the Norwegian and the English flag have been hoisted side by side. . . Hundreds of thousands of times Norwegian boats have been lying within range of English guns. Have they felt this as danger? No, on the contrary, they have felt it as a guarantee for just and noble treatment!"

If one wants to read something of the practical

chivalry of the sea during the Great War, he has but to go to records such as those quoted by Professor Dixon in his delightfully clear and vivid little book, "The British Navy at War." "A single lieutenant of the Naval Reserve," he says, "besides attending to other matters, destroyed forty or fifty mines, twice drove off an inquisitive German Taube, attacked an equally inquisitive Zeppelin, twice rescued a British sea-plane, and towed it into safety, rescued in June the crew of a torpedoed trawler, sixteen men, also the crew of a sunk fishing-vessel; in July assisted two steamers that had been mined, saving twenty-four of the sailors, in September assisted another steamer, rescued three men from a mined trawler, towed a disabled Dutch steamer, and assisted in rescuing the passengers; in November assisted a Norwegian steamer, rescued twenty-four men, and also a Greek steamer, which had been torpedoed, and rescued forty."

The love of fair play, which is an instinct with all true men of the sea, made the submarine particularly detested. "All the crew swallowed up in a minute," said a skipper in telling of the time when a torpedo hit one of his fellow-fishing-smacks. "They don't give you a chance to strike

out for your life or to know even that you 've
been done for in a fair fight.''

Therefore the decoy work of the ''Q'' boats, as
they were called, was pursued with enthusiasm
despite, perhaps because of, its great risks. The
story of His Majesty's ship *Pargust,* which, disguised as a merchant vessel, succeeded in luring
to its destruction an enemy submarine on June
7, 1917, may serve to illustrate the manner in
which the ''play-acting'' crews of the ''Q'' boats
worked. After the ship had been attacked by the
submarine, a portion of the men, playing the rôle
of ''panic party'' or sole survivors, put forth in
a life-boat and, acting in this way as lure, led the
submarine within fifty yards of the ship, which
then unmasked and opened fire. The submarine,
with oil pouring from her side and the crew
pouring from the conning-tower, seemed in a
desperate case. At first the crew held up their
hands in surrender, but when the fire from the
Pargust ceased, they apparently rallied and
made an attempt to escape under cover of the
heavy mist. Fire was reopened then until she
sank, only one officer and one man of the crew
being rescued. American destroyers and a British sloop appeared on the scene shortly after-

ward, and the decoy ship was towed in triumph to port. "As on previous occasions," it was stated, "officers and men displayed the utmost courage and confidence in their captain, and the action serves as an example of what perfect discipline, when coupled with such confidence, can achieve." One officer and one man from among them was selected by ballot for the award of the Victoria Cross.

But perhaps of all the gallant attempts to wrest the weapon of the submarine from the ruthless hand of the enemy the raid on Zeebrugge was the most daring. Ever since this Belgian port had been captured by the Germans in the autumn of 1914 it had been used as a base for submarines, destroyers, and aircraft. It was so situated that swift instruments of death could be thrust from their sheltered harborage and back again before the watchers of the sea had time to deal with them.

"If we could only destroy that scorpions' nest!" it was said. But how was it to be accomplished? The port was provided with heavy guns past all possibility of attack; no ships could approach under their raking fire. Moreover, it had the added defense of a crescent-shaped mole thirty feet high, which held the entire harbor within its fortified curve.

Yet there are no bounds to what men of the sea will dare in a great cause. "There *is* a way to destroy that harbor if we can block the channel by sinking some ships in just the right position," some one suggested. Plans were presented and discussed.

"It is possible," declared the commander. "The risk is great, but the object to be attained is greater. Given a dark night, with the sea and the wind favoring us, a storming party may reach the mole in a smoke screen without being observed. Then, effecting a landing, they may succeed in so engaging the attention of the enemy that block ships—three old cruisers filled with concrete—may be taken to the harbor and sunk there so as to completely fill the channel."

It was, as the German papers said in commenting on it afterward, a "fantastically audacious" scheme. But the chivalry of the sea does not count the cost when the call comes.

On the night of April 22, 1918, all conditions seemed as favorable as possible. Four antiquated British cruisers were chosen for the glorious attempt. Three of them were filled with concrete, and one, the *Vindictive*, working with two ferry-boats, *Daffodil* and *Iris*, was to land the storming party on the mole to surprise the enemy, and, if possible, destroy the guns, submarine depots, and sea-plane bases there while diverting attention from the main effort, the sinking of the block ships. Even the official report of the raid glows and tingles. Here is the Admiralty account of the approach of the storming party:

The night was overcast and there was a drifting haze. Down the coast a great searchlight swung its beam to and fro in the small wind and short sea. From the *Vindictive's* bridge, as she headed in towards the mole, with the faithful ferry-boats at her heels, there was scarcely a glimmer of light to be seen shoreward. Ahead, as she drove through the water, rolled the smoke screen, her cloak of invisibility, wrapped about her by small craft. This was the device of Wing-Commander Brock, without which, acknowledges the admiral in command, the operation could not have been conducted.

A northeast wind moved the volume of it shoreward ahead of the ships. Beyond it was the distant town, its defenders unsuspicious. It was not until the *Vindictive*, with bluejackets and marines standing ready for landing, was close upon the mole that the wind lulled and came away again from the southeast, sweeping back the smoke screen and laying her bare to the eyes that looked seaward.

There was a moment immediately afterward when it seemed to those on the ships as if the dim, coast-hidden harbor exploded into light. A star shell soared aloft, then a score of star shells. The wavering beams of the searchlights swung around and settled into a glare. A wild fire of gun flashes leaped against the sky, strings of luminous green beads shot aloft, hung, and sank. The darkness of the night was supplemented by a nightmare of daylight of battle-fired guns and machine-guns along the mole. The batteries ashore awoke to life.

As we read of the landing where the men swept on through the terrific fire of the German machine-guns while the wounded and dying raised themselves to cheer on their comrades, we know that there are indeed no limits to human heroism.

It is a significant fact that, as the bombing parties went on with their task of destroying the machine-gun emplacements, fortifications, and other military equipment of the mole, they took no prisoners. The Germans had immediately retired from the outlying defenses and contented themselves with dealing out death from their machine-guns on the shore. Indeed, they were so absorbed in watching from that point of vantage the annihilation of the presumptuous madman that the object of the raid was actually accomplished; the three block ships were successfully placed in the channel, a submarine was blown up in just the right place to destroy the viaduct that connected the mole with the shore, and the greater part of their brave crews were rescued. A leading German paper, in commenting on the affair, said: "It would be foolish to deny that the British fleet scored a great success through a fantastically audacious stroke in penetrating into one of the most important strongholds over which the German flag floats."

And so it was by sublime audacity and sublimer courage and faithfulness that the mariners of England kept at their task of keeping the seas until the hour of victory struck.

The day came when the German admiral appeared before Admiral Beatty to make arrangements for the formal surrender of the entire German Navy. "You understand that we are driven to this," he said. "Hunger leaves no choice." Then he presented a document which stipulated that the crews should be kindly treated.

"Tell them they are coming to England; that will be enough," said Sir David Beatty, tearing the document through as he looked full into the other admiral's eyes calmly, yet with a flash in his own, "like a North Sea storm."

On the day of the bloodless, inglorious surrender the German ships steamed out at last from their hiding—unscarred, unhonored, and unsung, and delivered themselves up to the victors.

FIGHTERS FOR PEACE

"I always told you," said Admiral Beatty, in acknowledging the resounding cheers of his happy mariners, "I always told you they would have to come out."

THE CHAMPION OF PEACE

PRESIDENT WILSON

I do not believe that it was fancy on my part that I heard
in the voice of welcome uttered in the streets of this great
city and in the streets of Paris something more than a personal welcome. It seemed to me that I heard the voice of one
people speaking to another people, and it was a voice in
which one could distinguish a singular combination of emotions. There was surely there the deep gratefulness that the
fighting was over.

Back of us is the imperative yearning of the world to have
all disturbing questions quieted, to have all threats against
peace silenced, to have just men everywhere come together for
a common object. The peoples of the world want peace and
they want it now, not merely by conquest of arms, but by
agreement of mind.

WOODROW WILSON: Speech at Guild Hall, London,
        December 28, 1918.

THE CHAMPION OF PEACE

From the very beginning of the terrible conflict between nations that we call the Great War, President Wilson was the champion of peace. He was no less that champion when he armed and led his people into battle than he was when he kept them out of war. In the dazzling moment of victory, when it was perhaps even more difficult to see clearly and act wisely than in the dark hour of struggle, he was still the voice of one crying peace.

But because this champion is a man of different stature from his fellows he has been an enigma both to his followers and his opponents. "To be great is to be misunderstood"; and perhaps the most bitter part is the inevitable misunderstanding of those who acclaim one master and guide, while giving no heed to the true meaning of his message. The voice of the champion of peace was lost at times in the clamor of the pacifists of various sorts.

I think we touch the heart and core of the diffi-

culty when we see that President Wilson is a
thinker. That is to say, he is fundamentally different in his reactions from the mass of men, who
live by instinct and feeling. Thought is too la-
borious a process for most of us, who have either
to work hard for a living or still harder to keep
ourselves happy and contented. The many will
always live by the light of the thought of the few.

It is not, however, as reason that new ideas win
men. It is only as thought is translated into life
and feeling that it has power. Then the truth
seen by the few leavens the whole mass and becomes the practical wisdom of the crowd.

The story of the champion of peace is the history of a man who had thought deeply on the vital
concerns of his nation suddenly thrust into the
position of world leader at a time when traditions and landmarks were swept away by the
overwhelming cataclysm of the most terrible war
that mankind had ever known. It is only as we
realize that he was facing the changing world
as a thinker at a time when most people were so
swayed by intense feeling that it was impossible
to see things from more than one angle, that we
have any key to the meaning of his leadership.

Those who have attempted biographical studies

THE CHAMPION OF PEACE

of Mr. Wilson are agreed that the thing of most
significance in the preparatory stage of his career was an article on "Cabinet Government of
the United States," which he wrote for a leading
review in 1879, the year he received his A. B. degree from Princeton. This paper, a carefully developed discussion of some eighteen pages, was
remarkable both for the foundation of solid schol-
arship on which it rested, and for its comprehen-
sive grasp and original thought. We know of
many instances where talent or genius outstrips
at a bound those who have toiled through long
years of effort, but it is usually in some field where
intuition and inspiration furnish the wings. It is
seldom that youth distinguishes itself by its
breadth of knowledge coupled with power of individual observation and analysis.

We find it, moreover, worthy of note that this
paper written in his undergraduate days was a
sort of preliminary sketch for the volume "Congressional Government: A Study in American
Politics," published several years later. This
analysis of legislative procedure by the House
of Representatives, the Senate, and the executive,
with particular attention to the part played by
Congressional committees, is not only important

in itself, but as it throws light on Mr. Wilson's habits of thought and his policies as President. We see, first, that he was willing to devote years of patient study to one subject; and, second, that, in so far as possible, he worked out in practice the things that he had presented in theory.

It is also significant that he spent nearly thirty years in his preparatory studies before he entered upon his work as a professor of history and political science; and this, in turn, was but a further period of preparation for his original, administrative work as an educator and statesman. Only a man used to proceeding by the slow, sure-footed way of deliberate, reasoned thought would have been content to go forward so painstakingly, waiting for the fullness of time for results.

Is it not strange that this President, who was above all else a man of peace, who asked for nothing but the chance to work out constructive plans for the betterment of our financial system, labor conditions, and the conservation of our national resources, should have been from almost the beginning of his term compelled to grapple with the problems of war? It was as if Fate said, "The time has come when your nation must be proved not in aloofness, but as a sharer of the fortunes

of other nations.'' In the days when the makers
of the republic talked about avoiding ''entangling
alliances,'' the oceans that swept the coasts of
America did, indeed, mean separation and protection. But modern discoveries and inventions,
with changed conditions of commerce, competition, and means of aggression, have compelled a
new policy. It is no longer possible for a nation
to live or die unto itself. As different peoples
won civilization when they realized that coöpera-
tion must supplant the law of the jungle, so now
the various nations were to learn that they were
of one kindred, and that only as they succeeded
in working out their salvation through mutual
forbearance and friendliness could the race of
men endure.

Mr. Wilson at once made it clear (as he had presented the matter in his ''Congressional Government'') that it was possible for a President to be
in effect a prime minister, initiating and directing
a definite plan of legislation as active, responsible head of his party, instead of leaving the control to irresponsible, but all-powerful, committees in Congress. The new order of things was
inaugurated and symbolized by the way in which
he revived the early practice of Washington and

Adams in appearing before Congress and delivering his messages in person, instead of sending more or less perfunctory documents to be read by the clerk. When Jefferson, who was not particularly happy as a speech-maker, set the precedent of written messages, the gulf between the legislative and executive branches of our government was definitely widened, and the defects of our system, as compared with the English democracy, where responsible executive heads are a part of the deliberative body, became in time more and more marked.

As we have seen, Mr. Wilson fully realized this defect in the way the check and balance system, as planned by the framers of the Constitution, had been altered in the practical working of our government, and he was determined to be a premier President, and insure an efficient, constructive handling of the promises laid down in his party platform.

"You have to admire the President for his stubborn courage if for nothing else," said a fair-minded opponent of the administration. "And when you consider that he is living up literally to principles he has held for some forty years you must admit that he has had time to form an

opinion. If the members of Congress had read
and marked his 'Congressional Government,'
they might have been less amazed by his 'czarism'
as they call it.''

For the feeling grew in the legislative branch
of the government that its prerogatives were being more and more usurped by the executive.
Members of the President's party were given definite instructions as to their proper action; when
some dared to oppose him and to obstruct important measures, their constituencies were in-
voked in the name of loyalty to the administration not to return the rebellious member. It was
said that the President was maintaining the discipline of a strict schoolmaster. Certainly he
held the whip hand, and by sheer force of will succeeded in putting through an extraordinary
amount of important legislation, despite the
clamor of sectional interests. Those who had declared that the Democratic party was so lacking in
coherence of policies and principles that they
could never carry through any really constructive
program were put to confusion.

But in the meantime the breach between Congress and the President widened. He was respected or feared by all; he was understood by

none. Even those who came into close touch with Mr. Wilson (and that was a privilege accorded to few) frankly admitted that they did not understand him.

A sentence or two which Mr. Wilson once wrote of Mr. Cleveland as President would seem to throw some light on his own attitude. "A certain tough and stubborn fibre is necessary (in a President), which does not easily change, which is inelastically strong." This "tough and stubborn fibre" was the more easily preserved because of Mr. Wilson's remoteness from personal contacts that might have subjected it to strain.

"To Washington the closed gates of the White House symbolize the President," says Maurice Low, in his biographical study. "The White House seems a place of mystery as great as Mr. Wilson himself . . . Seldom does the President ask any one to break bread with him. Even with the members of the cabinet there is almost no real intercourse. They transact their business with him, they see him as necessity or occasion demands, but intimacy does not exist. Mr. Wilson, after five years in the searchlight of a hundred million curious and inquisitive people, remains as remote, as unknown, as elusive a personality as if he belonged to another sphere.''

But the President's aloofness is itself a symbol. It is the outward sign of an inward difference that sets him apart from the mass of men. That difference, as has been already indicated, is the keynote to his character. "He is a straight thinker," said a man whom circumstances had brought in close touch with Mr. Wilson in recent years, "and straight thinking is so rare that it mystifies. Most men do not think, and the few who do have muddy thoughts. The President thinks straight, and his thoughts are clear.''

Most people were certainly mystified by the position Mr. Wilson took in face of the anarchy in Mexico. "Why does n't the United States step in and clean up that plague spot at our border, and safeguard the interests of Americans and American business?'' it was asked. The President was accused of weakness and indecision when he refused to adopt a policy of intervention to protect by force of arms the commercial adventurers whose enterprise had led them to cast in their lot with the Mexicans.

"Have not the European nations,'' said Mr.

293

Wilson, "taken as long as they wanted and spilled as much blood as they pleased in settling their affairs, and shall we deny that to Mexico because she is weak? No, I say. I am proud to belong to a great nation that says, 'This country which we could crush shall have as much freedom in her own affairs as we have.' "

Mexico, however, had no basis for understanding the nature of this toleration, which seemed to spell weakness (as it did to many in America), and her deliberate aggressions made it necessary for United States troops to enter that unhappy country. But after brief terms of occupation they were withdrawn, since the President steadfastly refused to make any difficulties a cause of war.

"I have faith that democracy will in spite of everything win its way," he said. "The stronger nation can afford to be patient. We are, perhaps, finding a chance of proving to the peoples of Central and South America that we stand for peace, and for the right of each nation, great or small, to free, unmolested development."

The President's policy in the Philippines also showed his faith in democracy, and made for peace. The desire of the islanders for a larger

294

measure of home rule was granted by replacing the Philippine Commission by an elected, representative body, and the guardian nation definitely put on record its pledge "to withdraw its sovereignty over the Philippine Islands and to recognize their independence as soon as a stable government can be established therein."

From the very beginning of his administration, Mr. Wilson had to deal with these perplexing foreign problems. The Mexican question had already reached a critical stage when he came into office. Feeling ran high. American lives had been taken; American property had been destroyed. Some strong action should be taken. War? Well, it might not come to that, but we should make the power of the United States felt in no uncertain way. The policy of "watchful waiting" was an exasperation.

"The President has no policy. He is an opportunist, steering no straight course, but depending on the wind of circumstance," it was said. So the President's faith and patience were read by many who could see the Mexican situation only from the angle of American problems and prejudices.

Have we not now the key to Mr. Wilson's attitude towards the European tragedy? Can we not understand in some measure even that strange appeal to the people to be neutral in the face of what many saw was a life or death struggle between freedom and ruthless autocracy?

"The United States must be neutral in fact as well as in name," he wrote, "during these days that are to try men's souls. We must be impartial in thought as well as in action; must put a curb upon our sentiments as well as upon every transaction that might be construed as a preference of one party to the struggle before another. . . .

"Shall we not resolve to put upon ourselves the restraint which will bring to our people the happiness and the great and lasting influence for peace we covet for them?"

Probably only to the President, champion of peace, and one who was accustomed to acting in accordance with the dictates of reason, not feeling, was such a neutrality possible.

America was, however, even less prepared for war in thought than in armies and munitions. The world it knew was built on foundations of peace and freedom for all. One could not even conceive the new order. Mr. Wilson, whose whole soul and every habit of thought cried out against

WOODROW WILSON
President of the United States

the appeal to force in the settlement of difficulties, saw only that the United States among all the nations must have the faith and the sanity to keep in the way of peace. For her own sake and for the saving help she might one day give to the stricken peoples of Europe, she must avoid entangling alliances.

He himself must face the situation soberly, taking time to weigh every factor. He saw that he had the responsibility of acting as guide and trustee to a divided nation. There were those—people for the most part in the Eastern States—who had formed the habit of looking in thought and sympathy across the Atlantic, who were stirred to the depths by the plight of Belgium and France, and who were convinced that civilization itself was threatened. Then there were the German-Americans, as they were called, some five million people born in Germany and Austro-Hungary, together with nine millions of German parentage. Between these two camps were those who for some reason—prejudice due to crude or false history teaching, or Irish sympathies—were hostile to England. German propaganda, moreover, was ceaselessly at work to foster suspicion of Great Britain and so to remove the chance of

297

understanding and alliance between the two great English-speaking democracies. It must also be remembered that those who had suffered through Russian oppression, the Jewish and Polish immigrants, for instance, were antagonistic to the Allies. Many Americans were, indeed, more or less suspicious of Russia, and all had been brought up to think only good of Germany. These facts must explain the various shades of opinion and prejudice that clouded the vision of well-meaning people in the early days of the war. The President saw the country divided into these distinct classes, and he saw a very large number from among all groups who were so content with the sudden tide of prosperity that the needs of the warring countries had brought to business of every kind that they asked only for a continuance of peace and the opportunity for profit. Surely neutrality was the only safe, the only possible course.

In the early days of the war, however, it was soon evident that nothing more than an impersonal, official neutrality could be preserved. American enterprise, sorely tempted by the price Germany was willing to pay for certain products, felt resentment against the British blockade which interfered with profits. On the other hand, American lives were lost by the piratical methods of German submarine warfare. We have heard it said that "money talks," but that "dead men tell no tales." It would seem as if for a time public sentiment in America gave point to these cynical proverbs, since more feeling was apparently aroused by the business losses than by the crimes of Germany. Carefully neutral notes of protest were sent to both powers, which had no effect except to produce irritation in the countries concerned. To England, who was using the legitimate weapon of siege against her enemies, it seemed that America thought only of the profiteering opportunity that the war gave. To Germany, helpless in the toils of the blockade, Americans were also a vulgar, profit-loving people, who were, moreover, guilty of the infamy of furnishing munitions to her enemies.

In her impotent fury she threw aside all regard for the laws of nations and of humanity. Working through the Germans in America, she plotted to destroy factories carrying contracts with Great Britain, and her crimes on the seas culminated in the sinking of the *Lusitania,* a great, floating hotel, filled with passengers belonging for the most part to a neutral nation. But the German torpedo that mangled this unarmed ocean liner, and sent it in a few minutes to the bottom, with twelve hundred innocent victims, did a greater, a more deadly work, of which those who celebrated the "triumph" in Berlin little dreamed. "All peoples—and the cowardly, dollar-loving Americans in particular—will think twice now before they defy the might of our Fatherland," exulted the disciples of "frightfulness."

It was indeed a "shot heard round the world," but somehow people did not quail and crouch as the Germans had anticipated. With all their science and philosophy, how little they understood other nations and the springs of human action! Even indifferent and unthinking people were now aroused to a realization of the German menace. The mobilization of America began at that moment.

All eyes were turned to the President. Consciously or unconsciously, the people of the nation were crying out for a leader. Even those who had acclaimed the champion of peace chiefly on the negative count that "he kept us out of war," felt that there must be in this crisis some strong expression of the outraged heart and conscience of humanity.

For a day or two the President was silent. Then, in speaking to a meeting of newly naturalized citizens in Philadelphia, he simply repeated a message that he had voiced on many other occasions in regard to the duty of Americans as a people with a mission:

"The example of America must be a special example," he said. "The example of America must be the example not merely of peace, because it will not fight, but of peace because peace is the healing and elevating influence of the world and strife is not. There is such a thing as a man being too proud to fight. There is such a thing as a nation being so right that it does not need to convince others by force that it is right."

Nothing could illustrate more completely the aloofness of the President from the natural feeling of people than this speech. When they asked for the bread of counsel and guidance he gave them this stone of self-righteous preachment!

It is easy, too, to understand the effect the one phrase, "Too proud to fight," had, when it was flashed over the wires to England and France,

301

countries who were giving their life-blood that freedom might not perish from the earth. If they did not say, "Those insufferable, dollar-serving Yankees actually have the effrontery to flaunt their selfishness as superiority!" it was because they were speechless with indignation.

It is clear, however, that this "blazing indiscretion," as one biographer of Mr. Wilson calls the "Too proud to fight" speech, illustrates not only the President's remoteness from the emotional reactions of his fellows, but also his preoccupation with his own train of thought. Looking before and after, can we not understand what he was trying to say to the people? America must testify to a faith in peace as the healing of the nations. A man can have such entire confidence in his cause that he feels it does not rest with his puny strength to establish it. He knows that the foundation principle of the universe, the law "that preserves the stars from wrong," is on his side. Can he not then be sure of the victory? Why should the unconquerable soul feel that it must rely on the weapons of flesh?

We cannot doubt that Wilson, the thinker, was striving to drive home some appreciation of this truth at a time when he saw that America must soon join the ranks of those who were fighting for peace. For he knew that Germany was surely, relentlessly, bringing the war to America, as she had to the democracies of Europe; and he felt that it must be his task to prepare his country to meet the stress of that time worthily, by fighting with all that was in her for a just peace. Never for a moment did he lose his hold upon the faith that peace was the only basis for the life of the nation as for the individual, but his speeches now sounded a new note of warning that all must stand ready to keep the peace by defending the right against ruthless might.

"We are peculiar in this," he said, "that from the first we have dedicated our force to the service of justice and righteousness and peace. But do you not see that, in guarding the honor of the nation, I am not protecting it against itself, for we are not going to do anything to stain the honor of our own country. I am protecting it against things that I cannot control, the action of others. And where the action of others may bring us I cannot foretell. You may count upon my heart and resolution to keep you out of the war, but you must be ready if it is necessary that I should maintain your honor."

FIGHTERS FOR PEACE

It was only too evident to those who were in a position to know something of what lay behind Germany's moves that she had consented to abate her terrorism on the seas merely to gain time while equipping herself with new and improved submarines. The President had every reason to believe that, as soon as she felt herself fully armed, she would once more defy America, the rights of neutral nations, and the laws of humanity. On the eve of that day, however, he made one last effort to lead the war-weary peoples to a permanent peace.

Addressing the Senate on January 22, 1917, he said in effect: Have not all, through suffering, come to a point where there can be a mutual agreement to forego immediate triumph for the great victory to all mankind that a permanent peace would mean—a peace based not on "balance of power, but a community of power?" Each side says that there is no desire to crush the other. Why not now come together and make that real by declaring for a "peace without victory," a stable, forward-looking peace that rests on the principles, first, of the right of all peoples great and small to their own national life, and a government deriving its authority from the consent of

304

the governed; and second, a league of free nations to adjust and settle differences, hence "the moderation of armaments, which makes of armies and navies a power for order merely, not an instrument of aggression or of selfish violence?"

Not even the President's "Too proud to fight" speech was more unpopular than this "Peace without victory" plea. To the Germans, who were confident of an early, sweeping success, it was only taken seriously as it seemed an indication of weakness. To the Allies, who had fought a hard fight for two and a half years against terrible odds, it seemed an unthinkable compromise with the forces of death and destruction. Only with the evasive pacifists, who seized as their slogan of the moment, "Peace without victory," did the speech find welcome. And to the President, who knew that the peace for which he was pleading, like all precious things, could only be won through travail and sacrifice, this unthinking acclaim must have been bitter, indeed.

This speech was the brave attempt of an idealist to lead the way to a practical application of the moral principles governing the lives of right-minded individuals and nations, to international problems. Surely that was at once idealism and common sense. Could civilization itself survive another such struggle, where the tooth-and-claw method was reinforced by the diabolic contrivances of modern science?

The President's plea was also a last effort to win Germany from her faith in the gospel of force and the divine right of the strongest, before sounding the call to arms. Never again would the chance for a peace by treaty be hers. When America was convinced that only in terms of force would her protests against aggression and inhumanity be heeded, there could be no end but that of unconditional surrender.

On January 31, 1917, when Germany announced her renewal of the submarine warfare, in effect closing the seas to the ships of neutral nations, the President at once severed diplomatic relations and asked Congress for authority to declare "a state of armed neutrality" existing against Germany. This meant arming merchant-ships and taking all precautions possible to protect American lives and American commerce. "I hope," he said, "that I need give no further proofs and assurances than I have already given throughout nearly three years of anxious patience that I am the friend of peace and mean to preserve it for

THE CHAMPION OF PEACE

America as long as I am able. I am not now proposing or contemplating war or any steps that
lead to it. I believe that the people will be willing
to trust me to act with restraint, with prudence,
and the true spirit of amity and good faith that
they have themselves displayed throughout these
trying months.''

Only a man who had thoroughly convinced the
American people that he had used every possible
honorable means of keeping peace could have led
a united nation into war. But when war was seen
to be inevitable there were no half-way measures.
America, convinced at last that force was the
only language that would be understood, could
use "force, force to the utmost, force without
stint or limit'' in order "to make the world safe
for democracy.''

In addressing the extra session of Congress on
the evening of April second, President Wilson
said in conclusion:

"It is a fearful thing to lead this great peaceful
people into war, into the most terrible and disastrous of all wars, civilization itself seeming to be
in the balance. But the right is more precious
than peace, and we shall fight for the things that
we have carried nearest our hearts, for democracy,

307

FIGHTERS FOR PEACE

for the right of those who submit to authority
to have a voice in their own governments, for the
rights and liberties of small nations, for a universal dominion of right by such a concert of free
people as shall bring peace and safety to all nations and make the world itself at last free.''

From the beginning, when the President declared for the principle of universal liability to
service as the only democratic and efficient means
of assembling an army, to his final determined
stand with the Allies for unconditional surrender,
the champion of peace stood for a vigorous pros-
ecution of the war—force to the utmost. But it
was always a forward-looking struggle, because
never for a moment did he allow the people to
lose sight of the great goal.

''The great fact that stands out above all the
rest,'' he said in his Flag Day address, ''is that
this is a people's war, a war for freedom and justice and self-government amongst all the nations
of the world, a war to make the world safe for
the peoples that live upon it and have made it
their own, the German peoples themselves included.

''For us there is but one choice. We have
made it. . . . Once more we shall make good with

308

THE CHAMPION OF PEACE

our lives and fortunes the great faith to which we were born, and a new glory shall shine in the face of our people.''

Striving to put the nation's purpose into concrete form, Mr. Wilson, in an address to Congress on January 8, 1918, laid down his famous "fourteen points" on which a just and lasting peace might be founded. "An evident principle," he said, "runs through the whole program I have outlined. It is the principle of justice to all peoples and nationalities, and their right to live on equal terms of liberty and safety with one another, whether they be strong or weak." The fourteen planks that the President held out for the building of a peace platform were at once the subject of query and debate. That was surely their purpose, to make people consider the question of proper material and the need of building. Also was it not with that purpose in mind that details and methods of adjustment were left for time to determine? But the cardinal principles of justice to all peoples and a guarantee of "their right to live on equal terms of liberty and safety with one another" through the formation of a protective league of nations shone out like beacon lights.

309

FIGHTERS FOR PEACE

Among the earnest and straight-thinking pacifists there were those who voiced the fear that in the intoxication of victory, America might become enamored with her own prowess and, forgetting her true mission, enter into competition with the other nations for power through armaments. And President Wilson, feeling that the moment of triumph was a time of testing no less critical than the hour of battle, decided to cast aside precedent and prejudice and go to confer face to face with those who would have the task of arranging the terms of peace.

"It must be as the prime minister, not as the chief executive of my nation, that I take part in the deliberation," he said to Premier Clemenceau.

We may perhaps find an indication of the positive influence of the champion of peace with kings and leaders as well as with the people of the Allied nations in these words with which the King of Italy welcomed him to Rome:

"Italy and America entered together into the war through a rare act of will," said King Victor Emmanuel; "they were moved by the purpose to concur with all their energies in an effort to prevent the domination of the cult of force in the world; they were moved by the purpose to re-affirm in the scale of human values the principles of liberty and justice. They entered into war to conquer the powers of war. Their accomplishment is still unfinished, and the common work must still be developed with firm faith and constancy for the purpose of effecting the security of peace.''